THEOLOGY
IN RED, WHITE, AND BLACK

BOOKS BY BENJAMIN A. REIST
Published by The Westminster Press

Theology in Red, White, and Black

Toward a Theology of Involvement:
The Thought of Ernst Troeltsch

THEOLOGY
IN RED, WHITE, AND BLACK

by
BENJAMIN A. REIST

THE WESTMINSTER PRESS
Philadelphia

Scripture quotations from the Revised Standard Version of the Bible are copyright, 1946 and 1952, by the Division of Christian Education of the National Council of Churches, and are used by permission.

Published by The Westminster Press®
Philadelphia, Pennsylvania

PRINTED IN THE UNITED STATES OF AMERICA

Acknowledgment for use of excerpts from copyrighted materials:

Doubleday & Company, Inc., from *Black Religion and Black Radicalism*, by Gayraud S. Wilmore. Copyright © by Gayraud S. Wilmore.

Grosset & Dunlap, Inc., from *God Is Red*, by Vine Deloria, Jr. Copyright © 1973 by Vine Deloria, Jr.

Harper & Row, Publishers, Inc., from "The Significance of the History of Religions for the Systematic Theologian," by Paul Tillich, in *The Future of Religions*, by Paul Tillich, ed. by Jerald C. Brauer. Copyright © 1966 by Hannah Tillich.

Johnson Reprint Corporation, from *The Soul of the Indian: An Interpretation*, by Charles Alexander Eastman. Houghton Mifflin Company, 1911.

The Macmillan Company, from *Custer Died for Your Sins*, by Vine Deloria, Jr. Copyright © 1969 by Vine Deloria, Jr.

The John G. Neihardt Trust, from *Black Elk Speaks*, by John Neihardt. Copyright 1932, 1959, 1961 by John G. Neihardt.

The Seabury Press, Inc., from *Liberation Theology*, by Frederick Herzog. © 1972 by Frederick Herzog.

The Viking Press, Inc., from *Book of the Hopi*, by Frank Waters. Copyright © 1963 by Frank Waters. All rights reserved.

Library of Congress Cataloging in Publication Data

Reist, Benjamin A.
    Theology in red, white, and black.

    Includes bibliographical references.
    1. Race (Theology)   I. Title.
BT734.R44   261.8′34′51   74-27936
ISBN 0-664-20723-5

To
Becky, Steve, and Burton

CONTENTS

PREFACE

I CANNOT REMEMBER WHEN THE CONCERNS THAT HAVE TAKEN shape in this discussion first came to dominate my attention, but I do know when and where the discipline and stimulus for attempting it originated. In 1968 I was elected to the Council on Church and Race of The United Presbyterian Church U.S.A., and since that time it has been my privilege to share both the trials and the joys of that company and its incomparable staff. Without the willingness of the brothers and sisters of that genuinely multi-ethnic circle to work patiently with me, I would never have seen what I have tried to formulate here.

The work on the research and writing lying behind this discussion began in the late summer of 1970, with the commencement of a sabbatical leave in 1970–1971. Dr. Raymond V. Kearns, Jr., then Associate General Secretary of the Commission on Ecumenical Mission and Relations, saw to it that I was appointed a consultant to the United Presbyterian delegation to the Uniting General Council of the World Alliance of Reformed Churches (Presbyterian and Congregational), meeting in Nairobi, Kenya, in August of that year. This made possible visits to Addis Ababa, Ethiopia, and to Accra, Ghana, as well as to Nairobi. Brief though it was, this trip to Africa was of tremendous significance in helping me gain an awareness of something of the background of the American black experience, both its past, and its present and future dimensions. More than that, and unexpectedly so, the trip was the occasion for my first real encounter with the present reality and promise of tribal thought, and thus it played a decisive role in the emergence of a growing sensitivity to the American Indian dimension of this present discussion. Dr. Kearns has been constant in his encouragement and interest as work on this project has unfolded.

Special gratitude is due to Dr. Gayraud S. Wilmore, whom it has been my privilege to know and work with for over twenty years. My high estimate of his *Black Religion and Black Radicalism* (1972) would be in place even if I had never known him, but the argument I have sought to develop in the discussion as a whole is indebted to his integrity and openness in ways beyond measure. Special gratitude is also due to Dr. Cecil Corbett, a Nez Percé Indian, who as a United Presbyterian minister is currently serving as Executive Director of Cook Christian Training School, in Tempe, Arizona. Along with the late Joseph Watson, Jr., a Navajo who served for several years as Associate for Indian Ministries of the Board of National Missions of The United Presbyterian Church U.S.A., he has given many hours to the running conversation that has helped me begin to understand American Indian religious and theological perspectives. Through Dr. Corbett and Mr. Watson I came to know, first in his writings and then in person, the remarkable Sioux, Vine Deloria, Jr.

The structure of the discussion emerged while I was preparing two lectures for presentation before the National Fellowship of Indian Workers, at Estes Park, Colorado, in June of 1972. In July of 1974 I once again addressed this body under the heading "American Indian Religious

Thought as It Relates to Christian Theology." Parts of Chapter II, Section C, and Chapter V, Sections B and C, informed these discussions.

Particularly in the early phases of the research and writing involved in this effort my colleague in the Graduate Theological Union of Berkeley, California, Dr. W. Hazaiah Williams, President-Director of the Center for Urban-Black Studies, gave indispensable encouragement and rich insight. I here record also countless conversations with my late colleague in the Department of Systematic Theology of San Francisco Theological Seminary, Dr. Cornelius O. Berry (1926–1973). Knowing the black experience from within, he contributed more than can be acknowledged to my own struggle to understand, during the four years we worked together.

The book would never have been completed without the peerless help of Thelma Furste, Faculty Secretary of San Francisco Theological Seminary.

BENJAMIN A. REIST

San Anselmo, California
July, 1974

THEOLOGY
IN RED, WHITE, AND BLACK

1:
THEOLOGY
AND HISTORIES

IN 1903, OVER SEVEN DECADES AGO, W. E. BURGHARDT
Du Bois began one of his most memorable books, *The Souls
of Black Folk*, with these words:

> Herein lie buried many things which if read with patience
> may show the strange meaning of being black here at the
> dawning of the Twentieth Century. This meaning is not
> without interest to you, Gentle Reader; for the problem of
> the Twentieth Century is the problem of the color line.[1]

The events of those seven decades, both in the life of Du
Bois himself (there for all to behold; he wrote no less than
four autobiographies!)[2] and beyond it, have surely proved
him correct. The trouble is that even on this side of the
Black Revolution, most white folks still refuse the cogency
of his observation.

This is especially true within the realm of theology.
Whatever else theology may be, it is the attempt to make
ultimacy intelligible. As such it always builds on myriad
prior cultural permutations in the never-ending effort to
discover fresh insights into the eternally powerful symbols
that the religions have bequeathed to us. On this side of the
Black Revolution, black scholars have taken up the task of
resisting the dominance of the white culture of the West in

this undertaking: and as we shall see, they have engaged in intensely constructive efforts. Some white scholars such as Frederick Herzog in his profound interpretation of the Fourth Gospel, *Liberation Theology* (1972), have shouldered their share of this burden; but it cannot be denied that theirs is a lonely task. *Why* this is the case is easy to state but complex in its implications.

From the white side, the decisive question raised by Du Bois inheres in his use of the definite article. Most whites are willing to concede immediately that *a* problem of the twentieth century is the problem of the color line. This, though, is not what Du Bois said; he said it is *the* problem of the twentieth century. He was right when he said it in 1903, and he is still right just over a decade beyond his death, when the century is three quarters spent. He was, in fact, right in far more convoluted ways than he could have known, for the problem of the twentieth century is the problem of the color *lines*. But there is only one way to move beyond him to the understanding of this remark, and that is to discern the depths of his use of the definite article.

What is centrally involved here is a question of *perspective*. What is also involved is the fact that it took the deepening of the civil rights movement of the 1950's and 1960's into the full-scale Black Revolution, *and* the accompanying fact that this triggered in turn the ethnic revolutions across the full mosaic that is humanity, to force this question into the open. The real root of racism is the question of perspective. The look of superiority on the face of a dominating white can yield as much pain—maybe more—than the overt brutality of a so-called red-neck. The shocking fact is that this look of superiority is more intractable on the face of the white liberal than it is on the face of some devoted servant of the Ku Klux Klan. For the white liberal is profoundly persuaded that whereas ethnic oppression is terrible, painful, destructive, and thus urgently awaits solution, it is nevertheless only one of a series of problems.

Precisely this condition is what Du Bois sought to unmask. For the ethnically oppressed, all of the so-called people of color, oppression is real, permanent, and unavoidable. It cannot be dislodged from the psyche by any maneuver, simple or complex. It is as constant as the breath of life itself. If every moment of respiration brings pain, the pain cannot be ignored; one can only live with it. Now, to be sure, white folks—millions of them—know such pain too. But many white folks know the term "oppression" only as a shorthand term for indicating vexatious components in an otherwise comfortable life. Even if the patterns of that vexatiousness are destructive, agonizing, wrenching, they *can* be dealt with without a fundamental change in the system itself. For such white people the problem of the color line is surely recognizable as *a* problem; but it is a *limited* problem—limited in the sense that no basic change in the patterns of human interrelationships need be won in order to alleviate it. This is what Du Bois denied, and this is what it took a Black Revolution, and all it has engendered, to expose. And in the light of this exposure one can at last get a handle on that highly emotional term "racism." A racist is one for whom ethnic oppression is one of a series of problems. A racist is one for whom Du Bois was profoundly wrong—*a* problem, not *the* problem, of the twentieth century is the problem of the color line.

In this light a crucial insight comes immediately to the fore. The most effective way to divert Du Bois' contention is to concede the point regarding the definite article but to expand the idea of racism into a generalization that is applicable to *all* struggles along the front of the color line. On this ground those of the ethnically oppressed who champion separatism can be conveniently termed "racists in reverse." This deliberately avoids, however, the decisive question of perspective. Ethnic separatists do not see the problem of the color line as *a* problem! Rather, they find the context of ethnic oppression so devoid of creative possibilities that withdrawal is the only alternative to the rage of outright nihilism. This may be despair, but it is surely not racism. Moreover, it may not be despair at all, but rather an immediate strategic necessity, providing time and room to gather and strengthen the insight and vision needed for the ongoing struggle. But this struggle, whatever its form, is not a struggle between contending racists. Rather, it is a struggle for liberation between those who know from within the urgency Du Bois so eloquently expressed, and their deadliest enemies, those who would reduce them to racists in reverse.

Thus the task at hand is to take up the perspective for which Du Bois contended, and to add to the efforts of others this present attempt to sort out its manifold implications. To reflect now in the light of Du Bois' insight is *not* to say that the problem of the color line is the *only* problem of the twentieth century. But it is to say that the color line is the problem that informs all other problems—quite a different thing. In the concluding section of *The Souls of Black Folk*, Du Bois set out a memorable treatment of the spirituals, calling them the "Sorrow Songs," the ultimate question being whether their undeniable hope, "a faith in the ultimate justice of things," [3] is justified. This poses the further question, "Would America have been America without her Negro people?" [4] And it speaks a hope, the blocking of which throughout the lifetime of this great man led to his leaving America and dying a citizen of Ghana:

> If somewhere in this whirl and chaos of things there dwells Eternal Good, pitiful yet masterful, then anon in His good

time America shall rend the Veil and the prisoned shall go free.[5]

Now no white American can read the lyrical intensity of this early work of Du Bois without being moved as to what could have been had he been heeded. But surely it is also the case that few white Americans are willing to *hear* and acknowledge the full range of the central element in his closing plea:

The silently growing assumption of this age is that the probation of races is past, and that the backward races of to-day are of proven inefficiency and not worth the saving. Such an assumption is the arrogance of peoples irreverent toward Time and ignorant of the deeds of men. A thousand years ago such an assumption, easily possible, would have made it difficult for the Teuton to prove his right to life. Two thousand years ago such dogmatism, readily welcome, would have scouted the idea of blond races ever leading civilization. So woefully unorganized is sociological knowledge that the meaning of progress, the meaning of "swift" and "slow" in human doing, and the limits of human perfectability, are veiled, unanswered sphinxes on the shores of science. Why should Aeschylus have sung two thousand years before Shakespeare was born? Why has civilization flourished in Europe, and flickered, flamed, and died in Africa? So long as the world stands meekly dumb before such questions, shall this nation proclaim its ignorance and unhallowed prejudices by denying freedom of opportunity to those who brought the Sorrow Songs to the Seats of the Mighty? [6]

History did not have to happen as it did. History need not continue as it is going. And maybe now—now that the shores of silence reverberate not only with the staccato sounds of terror but also with the calmer, even more devastating sounds of closely reasoned argument—maybe now we are ready to rend the veil so that *all* of God's children can be free.

Part of this task is theological in character. It may even transpire that one day we shall truly know that the *heart* of this task is theological in character. For the moment, though, that question must be left open. One need not be religious to buy into Du Bois' perspectival insight. Suppose, though, that one does come at the question he raises in the light of faith—then what? That such people exist, on both sides of the color line, is clear enough. And for all such people, whichever side of the line they are on, there is a common predicament that only recently has taken its decisive shape. The fact is that our ethics have outrun our theologies, and that this is the case for *all* involved. By no means is this the first time this has happened in the history of the Christian tradition. Indeed, the case is incontrovertible for the view that *every* significant move ahead in the realm of theological reflection has been the result of just such occurrences.[7] At any rate, this is a fair way to state what has happened now, and the works with which we shall be preoccupied throughout the body of this discussion can be taken seriously only in this light. For what we shall be pondering throughout this entire line of reflection is really a simple question. What happens to theology, from any side, when it takes up its task on the assumption that Du Bois was right, that *the* problem of the twentieth century is the problem of the color line?

To put the question this way will force into the open a deep and abiding fact about the nature of the Christian tradition, and we will be well advised to give it at least a provisional formulation here at the outset of our reflection. We have never known the gospel apart from its mixture with cultural forms. The gospel is not available as an abstraction. Surely, this must be so if the astonishing promise of *God-with-us, Emmanu-el,* is true. The problem which is ours to unravel, given the act of involvement with us by the God and Father of our Lord Jesus the Christ, is the problem of Christ and cultures. The trouble is that we invariably put that phrase in the singular, and thus miss the fact that the fascinating and terrifying issue, and therefore the productive one, is the question of Christ and culture*s,* not Christ and culture. Leave the phrase in the singular, and inexorably the dominance of prior cultural arrangements remains unchallenged and intact, with the result that the proclamation of the gospel deteriorates into the ideological propagation of some prior understanding of how the uniqueness of the Christ is to be known and understood.

Central to the question of Christ and cultures is the question of *theology and histories.* Here too we must pluralize a phrase we are accustomed to ponder in the singular. Only so can we discover and then confront the manner in which theology can and does dwell within, and strengthen, the domicile of racism. The most penetrating way to understand the racist mentality is to grasp its absolutizing of prior historical developments. The decisive issue for the attempt to think theologically in the light of Du Bois' perspectival insight is the issue of theology and histories. This is the threshold we must cross if we are to begin to live constructively beyond the fact that our ethics have outrun our theologies. Why so? How so?

Involvement in the civil rights movement inexorably yielded involvement in the Black Revolution and all it has engendered. Those from all sides of the color line who were caught up in the initial struggle concurred that the time had come for massive effort to deal with racial injustice. But what was uncovered as the struggle intensified was the historical component that deeply informed the very patterns of injustice. If, then, the historical issue was not rectified, the patterns would continually reduplicate themselves, for in the received tradition of the nation resided the unfolding assumption that liberty was the gift won by white culture, and to be bestowed by it on those it welcomed. Here, then, was the locus of a new and unexpected trauma of such whites as those whose ethical involvement would not permit their withdrawal from a struggle that increasingly identified *them* as the enemies of the oppressed. They could not live out their ethics without perpetuating the historical roots of the patterns of oppression! For those whites whose ethics have a theological origin the continuing problem is particularly excruciating: *If* we share the gospel; and *if* we understand it *at depth* as it has been transmitted to us; and *if* my birthright, but not yours, resides in the cultural matrix out of which it has come to each of us; and *if, furthermore,* neither you nor I are willing to see that it can be fathomed in terms of your cultural history as well as mine—*then* the mere proclamation of the gospel by either of us denies the integrity, the reality, the potential of you, and in this sense feeds your long dying, a dying I help effect.

Such a syllogism embodies the new theological problem that the ethnic revolutions of America have generated.[8] Its resolution demands *new* theological effort. A gospel that transcends *all* histories can be stated in terms of *each*. We really do not yet know what it means to say this. We only know that we must attempt to find out what it does mean. In so doing we must wrestle with issues that have a hoary past, but we will, at the same time, encounter astonishingly new questions—questions that may be the bearers of the presence of the Eternal One in our midst.

Hence this attempt at theology in red, white, and black. These are not all the hues that make up the full mosaic that is humanity. The attempt is a beginning only, envisioning the unfolding one day of theology in red, white, black, brown, and yellow, against the background of the blue earth, our mother. But the process must begin with the attempt at a theology in red, white, and black. For these are the historic American components of that full mosaic that is humanity, all of which is now present in this land. These are the three components that initially became indigenous by way of a tragically brutal but nevertheless irreversible process. Red brothers and sisters were already here when white brothers and sisters invaded and overwhelmed their sacred lands, with an invincible, imperial, and colonizing might built on the breaking backs of their enslaved black brothers and sisters.

We hear much talk these days of an American theology. None worthy of the name will ever emerge unless it has its beginnings as a theology in red, white, and black. And none can ever take a shape that would espouse a new chauvinism if it is born in the mosaic of humanity. America knows its own unique version of the nightmare of oppression. An American theology, then, dares not to palm off the American past as dreaming innocence. It seeks, rather, the atoning redemption of a new tomorrow, one in which its own unique composite could be of help in the dawning brotherhood and sisterhood of *all* God's children, all over his blue earth, who seek in whatever way to know him and love him by knowing, loving, and serving each other. This is the sense in which we must now try what has not been tried, and this is the sense in which our present discussion seeks only to prepare the way for a collective effort—a stride toward that coming Kingdom of God in which liberation shall be the bond that unites us all.

Words of caution and words of discipline are necessary as we embark on this task. The attempt is an attempt at a theology in red, *white*, and black. Nothing is to be gained by using the word "white" pejoratively. The problem is not that white theology is intrinsically evil. The problem is rather that the theological tradition, with the habits of centuries of accumulated efforts, has completely forgotten its own ethnic character. What we now know is a theological imperialism that is more aptly designated "North Atlantic Theology." The prevailing style of theological reflection in America has always been informed by the process of importing and transmitting ideas that originate in Europe, a process as evident in Roman Catholic thought as it is in the thought of the traditions of the daughter churches of the Reformation. What dominates American theological reflection is not *white* theology, but European-American theology, "North Atlantic Theology." The promise of theology in red, white, and black is that this dominance can be broken. Even in saying this, one must take care lest the attempt prove to be either shallow or ephemeral or both. North Atlantic Theology both has given, and still has to give, indispensable contributions to the journey we must now take. But now its *control* of the American theological enterprise must be shattered. In the process of moving toward a theology in red, white, and black, Americans whose ethnic roots are in Europe have the opportunity of becoming what they have never been—white! White, that is, not as lords and masters of history and the gospel, the automatic heirs of the chief seats in the great parliament of humanity, but white as one ethnic entity among the five that comprise the mosaic, *all* of which is in the image of God. To become white in the context of this attempt is precisely analogous to becoming black and becoming red in the context of this attempt—for what is taking shape is a future whose reality we can only dimly perceive now, but which we can anticipate with joy, since it will be comprised of all the components of the mosaic. Liberation for white brothers and sisters is precisely analogous to liberation for *all* the brothers and sisters—for them it means becoming white, not as the epitome of humanity in general, but as one component in the full mosaic. The mosaic will be beautiful only if all its colors are beautiful. It took the travail of the Black Revolution to open the way toward a future that no one save God controls.

Our theological task now is a task of *triangulation*—we must think our way around the red/white/black triangle, with insights from all sides of the triangle being considered on an absolute par. It is urgent that we do so now. It has always been urgent, and the task should have been undertaken long ago. But it is *possible* to undertake this task now—possible in a way it has never been before, possible in terms of an astonishing fact that we in our own time can only begin to appreciate. That fact is that the Black Revolution and all that it has yielded represents the *completion* of the American Revolution.[9] What happened two centuries ago was that the *white* component of the mosaic of American humanity succeeded in wresting its liberation from the hands of the European world whence it came. That victory was only partial—it effected the liberation of only one of the components of America's ethnic pluralism, the white component. And this remained, and remains, the dominating overlord of the red and black (and brown and yellow) worlds within the American scene. The American Revolution will not be complete until liberation is known across the whole spectrum of humanity present within the new world. The struggle in the streets of these latter years, then, has in fact been the struggle for the completion of the American Revolution. America's ethnic revolutions have to do with the extension of freedom.

That America's *theology* has never been truly liberated is

rooted in this incompleteness of the American Revolution. Restricted as it was in the sense in which we can now see this, the American Revolution left intact the virtually exclusive dependence of the American theological enterprise on its European prototypes. Not until the time that liberation of America's ethnic plurality approaches reality will this dependence become tenuous. Precisely this is what has now occurred. There exists for the first time, on *this* side of the Black Revolution and all that it has generated, an extant body of theological reflection that diverges, deliberately and vigorously, from the cultural myopia and ethnic singularity that has always characterized American theological reflections. Thus the process of theological triangulation of which we speak *can* be attempted now in a way that could not have been envisioned as recently as a decade and a half ago. That more—much more—will come from the labors of the theological intelligentsia of the ethnically oppressed is obvious. And that this intelligentsia is not newly born will become explicitly evident as we proceed. (Indeed, one of the most unenlightened forms of racism would be the assumption that blacks and reds began to think for the first time in the late 1960's!) Even so, the urgency of long-overdue questions is now accompanied by a genuinely new possibility of their being taken seriously. The ethnic revolutions are not confined to the streets, and they do not thrive on confrontation alone. They have already begun to yield broadening and deepening theoretical results that include decisively new crystallizations of insight into the intrinsically multi-ethnic effort to discern and to serve that liberating ultimacy for which all humanity seeks. The question is, Can these new insights be responded to from the white side in such a way that white insights are transmuted from informants of oppression into contributions to a shared, liberating future? Can there emerge a white theology that also bears the marks of a new, revolutionary perspective?

This process of theological triangulation is proleptic. One day—not far off—it will become *pentangular*, so to say (the *pentagram* being preferable to the *pentagon* for symbolic purposes, since the latter term is hopelessly besmirched for Americans!). *Brown* and *yellow* theological crystallizations must be at hand before the triangle can become a five-pointed star. These are imminent, but nascent. The dream is that the attempt at a theology in red, white, and black will facilitate their even more rapid emergence, just as the ethnic revolutions have brought new consciousnesses to each of these vibrant realms.

A crucial clarification is in order at this point. Clearly, in the phrase on which the title of this discussion turns, the terms "red," "white," and "black" each point toward complex, multidimensional realities. They are intelligible symbols, however, whose use is viable. The terms "brown" and "yellow" also refer to internally plural realms, but here the heterogeneity is even more diverse. Each of these ethnic components refers to more recent arrivals in the ethnic pluralism that constitutes the American scene, and by comparison the other three are indigenous. Like their black and red comrades, both brown and yellow brothers and sisters know brutal histories of ethnic oppression. But unlike their black and red comrades, they are only now breaking beyond a sense of cohesiveness that is confined simply to resistance to white racism. Puerto Ricans and Chicanos, for example, each know the condescending blindness of white Americans who dementedly assume that all brothers and sisters whose mother tongue is Spanish think alike. Accordingly, in the context of the struggle against ethnic oppression, they are thrown into a curious relationship born of a common enemy. And on the other hand it is proverbial that to white eyes "all Orientals look alike"; thus the noetic device caught up in the term "Asian American" has the staggering task of comprehensively unifying at least five discrete groupings: Chinese Americans whose roots and sympathies are with Taiwan, Chinese Americans whose sense of identity is more aptly focused with the word "Peking," Japanese Americans, Korean Americans, and Filipino Americans (whose inclusion in the term "Asian American" is obviously an absolute necessity, but who only in the sense of this construct can be thought of as part of the *yellow* component of the mosaic that is humanity). From the *brown* and the *yellow* sides of the pentagram will come the incisive crystallization of those who have already thought and lived their way into plural composites *from within.*

Already these insights are beginning to take shape.[10] To await their full fruition, however, would be to espouse unconscionable delay in the face of the combination of long-standing urgency and radically new possibility now before us. Thinking theologically around the red/white/ black triangle, however, will be valid only if it is construed as a necessary step toward the realization of the liberation of the full mosaic that is humanity. An America that has joyfully become red, white, and black can only welcome brown and yellow brothers and sisters into its midst. Contrariwise, an America that still refuses to embrace the unique composite that is centuries old, but has yet to be celebrated, will contain all, including its brown and yellow sons and daughters, in the same practiced hostility that means the death of each. The triangle is the necessary clue to the pentagram. A theology in red, white, and black is fragmentary, not in the sense of lack of wholeness but rather in the sense of anticipation.[11]

o   o   o

To wrestle with theology in the context of ethnic pluralism is to struggle with a problem that is not new, even though we are not accustomed to thinking of it as we now must. The problem of theology and histories is as old as the Biblical witness itself, and surely in our present century it has received a fresh articulation that can never be undone. The churches have moved closer together than any of them ever dreamed possible. The decisive issue in what we have known as the rise of *ecumenism* has to do with the historical character of *all* theological reflection. However the long-standing debate concerning the relationship between Scripture and tradition is settled, the undeniable fact is that no one can come to terms with the gospel of Jesus the Christ without reckoning with the historical process by which this gospel has been transmitted to the present. What has come into its own since the midpoint of the twentieth century is a new, and surely welcomed, recognition by all concerned that the variety and diversity of the historical components comprising the Christian tradition were and are relatable, and that, wherever this is pursued, salutary results have been enjoyed by all involved.

So it has come to pass that a spirit of openness succeeded in bridging the deep chasm wrought by the internal explosion that was the Protestant Reformation. Developing along with this has been an increasing sense of understanding within the multiplex realities connoted by the terms "Catholicism" and "Protestantism." The more the traffic across the bridge has increased, the more the conversation within the two realms has deepened, and vice versa. Indeed, the historians of some distant tomorrow will have a difficult time sorting out just which caused which (and it is somewhat comical to note that each side can make a case for the claim that its own internal developments triggered the whole movement).

It may well prove to be the case that one of the truly significant outcomes of the rise of ecumenism, both in America and beyond it, is the fact that theology is now capable of thinking its way into the far-reaching implications of what it means to live and believe in the context of ethnic pluralism. Theologians who have learned how to look beyond the frontiers of their own certainties cannot arrest this incurable curiosity once it has taken hold. Like it or not (and some, perhaps many, do not), to be a theologian on this side of the rise of ecumenism is already to have begun to come to terms with theological pluralism. What this means is not that some new homogeneity is now unfolding. What it means, rather, is that histories that have been either ignored or derided are now respected, probed, and (above all) *used* in constructive efforts to understand anew, and more deeply, the gospel of Jesus the Christ that is at the heart of the being of all the churches. The better the churches have understood each other the better they have understood themselves.

It is in this mood, and against this backdrop, that the attempt at a theology in red, white, and black unfolds. Much that we already should know will be operative here. Much, though, that we have regarded as sure and certain will undergo radical testing and radical reformulation—and some of it will collapse entirely, for that is always the counterpart of new patterns of relationship. In any event, in taking up the specific task of theological triangulation now before us we are not moving in totally unprecedented ways. We are rather insisting that the ecumenical experiment which is now irreversible will prove to be valid only if it is radically extended. For Americans, the place to begin this extension is at home. For while it is in its own way thrilling to live in a time when the ancient hostilities between Catholic and Protestant, and the combative condescensions between Catholic and Catholic, and Protestant and Protestant, are being transcended, it is at the same time tragic to acknowledge that red, white, and black continue to be related in terms of oppression. Here too, transversing the many-faceted reality of the churches, are histories that must be respected, probed, and built into a new constructive effort to transcend not just divisions, but destruction, in the hope not just of new understanding, but of the liberation of all humanity. Even theology in an ecumenical era must move drastically farther than it has thought possible if this is to happen.

The argument of our discussion will proceed along the lines of what, at this point, may simply be denoted as the dynamics of theological pluralism. No claim is made for the comprehensive finality of these particular sets of ideas. They have arisen inductively in the attempt to order the process of exchange and movement which a theology in red, white, and black must hold as its true goal. As we proceed we shall see that a sequential regimen is in operation, that these four dynamics unfold in a logical order, and that the refinements of each of them make sense only as the material at hand is carefully and reflectively scrutinized. But beyond this no further claim is made, except one. The principles of theological pluralism must be inductive. That is, they must emerge as the task itself proceeds. Otherwise true openness to unanticipated conclusions is not present. The theologically plural conversation is a conversation that must be *free*, free to discover what it did not know ahead of time, free to devise the ordering of its agenda, free to move beyond what it thought would be the marks of the integrity of its inquiry. In this mood, the dynamics of theology in the context of ethnic pluralism are at least fourfold.

1. *Mutual Intelligibility.* The point can be stated simply enough. *The* initial task of theology in the context of ethnic

pluralism is the task of effecting mutual understanding. This has all the appearances of being a mild point of departure. It is not. The fundamental reason why it took the Black Revolution and all that it generated to force the dawning of a new day is that white liberals assumed that they already grasped the issues at hand. Some whites still cannot understand why the word "integration" is no longer useful in the struggle for liberation. The effort to move beyond this impasse, though, discloses its own surprise. There are deep currents of reflection within the white theological world that have yearned for a fulfillment that *only* the struggle for ethnic liberation can truly bring. Mutual intelligibility is a matter of disciplined openness. It presupposes that time and effort are requisite for shared understanding.

2. *Mutual Interdependence.* Here the point cannot be stated so simply, for here we begin to encounter the real resistance of racism. Here is the point at which the decisive barrier of what we have called North Atlantic Theology must be overcome. Its *stranglehold* on the theological process must be broken once and for all. Here, too, is the point at which the basic reason why it is a mistake to equate *"white theology"* with North Atlantic Theology also reaches clarification. North Atlantic Theology is not *white*, not yet! For those whose roots are deeply embedded within it—and that is the great majority of us—the problem is to recognize that one cannot become white without recognizing one's dependence on the rest of the mosaic that is humanity for one's own self-understanding. Precisely this is what the tradition of North Atlantic Theology is loath to admit. The generalization is risky, of course, but irresistible nevertheless: North Atlantic Theology learns from no one but itself. For the theologians of the ethnically oppressed it has only nodding, paternalistic smiles, at best. Interdependence,

mutual interdependence, comes hard for those trained in its ranks, and this is exactly what must be overcome. Far more than discipline is at stake here. *Promise* is also involved, the promise of reciprocal creativity. But this promise will never be known apart from the deepest reaches of the genuine dependence of each upon all.

3. *Varying Rates of Relatability.* This mark is not at first apparent. Indeed, it is perhaps so subtle that it is likely to be missed, though, once seen, it can never be ignored. The process at hand is a process of *triangulation,* and accordingly, the conversation involved is not simply dialogical. Dialogue is intrinsic to the effort, of course, and that in the most unlimited sense. But *more* than dialogue is involved. The components of a genuine pluralism relate differently, at varying rates, with fluctuating tempo being the norm rather than the exception. One is tempted to think that this is true in general. One *knows* it to be the case in terms of the red/white/black triangle. So crucial is this that it can be flatly asserted that without it a theology in red, white, and black is not possible. For in this pluralism, if not in all, the fact is that if the rates of relatability are constant, someone is still dominating the exchange. Only those convinced of the intrinsic superiority of their own cultural heritage could ever assume that all either can or should relate in the same way.

4. *Mutual Openness to Change.* That change is the constant characteristic of theology in the context of ethnic pluralism ought to be expected. The question is, is it expected eagerly, are *all* open to it? The wonder of the new, the unanticipated, has always been there where theology has been done properly. The great giants of the tradition have exhausted their vocabularies trying to communicate the unfinishable character of the theological task. Even so, is there not a fresh compulsion in this direction in

the presence of the task now before us? A theology in red, white, and black must embrace and celebrate the ethnic plurality of humanity. The unity of humanity is the unity of a mosaic. Is it not the case, then, that the future of theology as we have known it is radically open? The question of the uncontrollable future is before us with an unnerving but invigorating intensity—for all who struggle with the depths of liberation. God—not his creatures—rules tomorrow's reflection upon this ultimacy.

A theology in red, white, and black could emerge along the path indicated by these four marks. If it does, it will have recognized that the problem of theology and histories has always been the peculiar gift of the God and Father of us all. His kingdom, for which his Son lived, died, and was raised from the dead, may be closer when brothers and sisters of all hues proclaim their gospels and listen to newly heard responses, not in order to conquer, but in order to relate.

2:
THE DISCIPLINE
OF MUTUAL INTELLIGIBILITY

THAT MUTUAL INTELLIGIBILITY IS A MATTER OF DISCI-pline becomes evident only when *each* word in the phrase is given the same emphasis. What is at stake is this: Listening in order to *relate* must be radically distinguished from listening in order to *conquer.* Everything depends on this. Theology in red, white, and black must begin here. Our first task is to bring this into sharp focus as an initial demonstration of what is entailed in the process of theological triangulation that we are proposing. We shall begin with the white side of the triangle, not because it is normative, but because one of the most restive and astute white theologians of the present century was preoccupied with concerns that receive both concrete corroboration and drastic extension in the context of America's red/white/black triangle. When we place alongside his insights something of the thought of two of the most incisive thinkers in the struggle for ethnic liberation today, one black, the other red, both his case and each of theirs gain depth and cogency.

A. *The Question of Mission*

Ernst Troeltsch (1865–1923) was *the* pioneer theologian in the attempt to take seriously the rise of the social sciences. His close association with Max Weber (1864–1920) became the entrée into his thought of the new discipline that Weber and others were shaping. This informed in depth the broad question to which Troeltsch's thought as a whole was addressed: Whither Christianity in the midst of the modern world? Troeltsch wrestled with this question with a deepening commitment to the view that its answer may *not* be assumed as self-evident. Indeed, he put the matter so forcefully that we may well regard him as among the first to attempt to break through, from within, the limits of what we have called North Atlantic Theology. Of the host of ways in which this happened, none is more significant for us than his attempt to transmute the understanding of the mission of Christianity to the non-Christian world.

As Troeltsch saw it, the question of mission has a built-in dilemma for modern Christians. On the one hand, faith cannot live without the compulsion to grow. It cannot be itself without seeking to expand. On the other hand, prior understandings of what this means are now called radically into question. A former time—indeed, all former times—could beg the question of differentiating the non-Christian world, and thus could regard all non-Christians as equally lost and condemned. "Today, for historically trained men, this is impossible," he wrote. Consequently, "the most simple and urgent motivation of the mission, the duty of sympathy and rescue" has fallen away. For such men "it is not a question of rescue, but of an uplifting to something higher; not conversion, but elevation." [1] So he wrote in 1913. A decade later, at the end of his life, he put the matter even more forcefully:

> The great religions appear to be just the crystallizations of the great racial spirits [*Rassengeister*], as similarly the races

themselves are the crystallizations of biological-anthropological forms. Between them there is not conversion and transformation, but agreement and understanding.[2]

At least two key insights from the massive complexities of Troeltsch's scholarly labors need to be known if we are to plumb the depths of what we have just heard him say. The first of these emerged from his debate with the celebrated historian of doctrine, Adolf von Harnack, concerning the *essence* of Christianity. The debate arose because of a set of lectures given by Harnack in 1900. (These lectures were destined to become as famous as Harnack's weighty treatises on the history of doctrine, and are still available in English translation under the title, *What Is Christianity?*)[3] Harnack had deliberately used for his lectures the title of Ludwig Feuerbach's controversial, but nevertheless equally celebrated, discussion of 1841, *Das Wesen des Christentums* ("The Essence of Christianity"). He did so because his explicit effort was to delineate his own understanding of what the heart of Christianity contains. The process he used to accomplish this, however, raised severely critical questions for Troeltsch. The burden of Troeltsch's critique of Harnack is really quite simple: The *essence* of Christianity may only be described, it may not be defined. If it is *defined,* an inexorable process of reduction sets in, whereby Christianity is given a singular, normative formulation. This is ahistorical, then, because it does not take into account the convoluted, contingency-ridden historical continuum out of which every attempt to describe the essence of Christianity emerges. When this historical continuum is given its due, one beholds a multitude of such attempts, all of them valid in their own way. This led Troeltsch to an inescapable conclusion:

Thus the "essence" can only be understood as the productive new interpretations and new adaptations of the historical

Christian power, corresponding to any total situation at any given time. The essence is different for each epoch, resulting from the totality of its influence.[4]

The conclusion Troeltsch reached on this matter was one he never deserted. It epitomizes the argument that received massive demonstration in the work by which he is best known, *The Social Teaching of the Christian Churches* (1912). More than that, though, it points toward the second key insight at the heart of his struggle with the question of mission. This has to do with his concept of the *historical individuality*, the idea that dominated his thought throughout the culminating decade of his labors.

The concept of historical *individuality* was one of the two basic themes Troeltsch pondered at length in his second, and final, major work, *Der Historismus und seine Probleme* ("Historical Relativism and Its Problems"). The other theme was the concept of development, and as the work progressed (it took him ten years to write the book) it became clear to him that the former ruled the latter.[5] What he sought to expound in this work was the manner in which modern man must learn to live with "the fundamental historicizing of all our thought about man, his culture and his value." [6] We must be clear on what he did not mean, in order to grasp what he wished to say here. He *did not* mean historical *determinism* (the sense in which "relativism" is often taken); he *did* mean historical *conditioning* (the sense in which the term "contextualism" could be used). Historical determinism represented for Troeltsch a hopelessly confused idea, rooted in the fallacious assumption that the laws of natural science can be simply applied to the problematic of historical investigation. This can be caustically rejected on the grounds that it failed to come to terms with the pivotal factor in history—the operation of vacillating, living *humanity*. Historical conditioning, however, he could not dismiss. If human creativity by its very nature defies any simple containment by the laws of natural science, at the same time and for the same reason it asserts the necessity of reckoning with the historical contexts that yield it. How else is its operation to become discernible? Moreover, all attempts to interpret the facts of history are as conditioned by context as the facts themselves. Against this background Troeltsch's concept of historical individuality gained its increasingly clear shape, focusing the passion for concreteness that informed all of his historical research.

> The decisive point is above all the *individuality* of historical forms and the objectivity aspired to in the entire investigation, to measure each form above all only in its particular will and content.[7]

When we hear Troeltsch insist that between the great religions there cannot be conversion and transformation, but only agreement and understanding, it is the concept of historical individuality that is informing his remark. Indeed, it was in the essay from which this is drawn, one of his last lectures, entitled "The Place of Christianity Among the World Religions" (*Die Stellung des Christentums unter den Weltreligionen*) that he developed his most penetrating use of this idea. He insisted, now, that it must be understood as governing all history, for history is a seething ferment, not at all reducible to singular sets of obvious guidelines, but rather invariably characterized by a panorama of unique, unfolding entities, each manifesting origins and promises of its own, and each convoluted with manifold expressions only abstractly unifiable, but nevertheless knowing internal coherence. This has a profound meaning and a twofold significance for Christianity. *Close in*, so to speak, it means that the very term "Christianity" must be understood as an abstraction, for it is itself a composite entity with an internal and reduplicating diversity, and this is in fact the very root of its creativity. Here what he had first seen in the exchange with Harnack regarding the essence of Christianity yielded its choicest fruit. *Farther out,* so to say, it means that at least the way toward a new future in the relationship between Christianity and the great world religions becomes clear. For this is a relationship between historical individualities which cannot ever be expected to disappear, but which can be expected to discover utterly unanticipated realizations of long-germinating potentialities. In his day Troeltsch could only glimpse this fascinating horizon, which is probably why he put the decisive conclusion negatively:

> This is the general law of history, that the divine reason or the divine life in history reveals itself in always new and always special individualization, and for that very reason it aims not at unity and universality, but at the ascent of each individual sphere of life to its present and highest possibilities. Above all, this law makes it impossible to designate Christianity as the unity and goal of [all] historical forces, [and] it makes it impossible to grasp Christianity itself as anything other than an historical individuality.[8]

We can follow Troeltsch no farther, for this is where he finished, and we are, or should be, far beyond him now. We dare not leave him, though, without taking seriously his parting word. The progression through which he moved must surely make it clear that his struggle with the question of mission was informed neither by caprice nor by cynicism. This struggle *can* be understood as yielding only a counsel of despair. But this is to misread Troeltsch, for he was not writing out the marching orders for the ultimate and final retreat. Quite the contrary, he was envisioning a new, utterly unprecedented exploration into unknown terrain:

> All that is clear is that it [Christianity] stands in a critical hour of its development and that here very basic and daring innovations are necessary, which go beyond all hitherto existing denominations.[9]

The polarity he discerned was the opposition between *conversion/transformation*, on the one hand, and *agreement/understanding*, on the other. Whether we like it or not, we now inhabit what was his far horizon. "Mutual intelligibility" is our term for what he referred to as "agreement and understanding." Perhaps his only error was the restriction of "conversion" to the level of a mere synonym for "transformation," and the reading of each of these terms in strictly pejorative fashion. In so doing, what he meant to reject was the attempt to obliterate all historical individualities except one, and the transformation of all into inhabitants of one composite. What he could not yet know was the dawning of an even deeper realization: When varying struggles to make ultimacy intelligible know an interfacing set of concerns, *conversion* is a distinct possibility, but it can only be a conversion that is *shared*. To seek what this means is to know Troeltsch's summons for "very basic and daring innovations" not as an option, but as a necessity. White theology of this sort can contribute to a theology in red, white, and black.

B. *Black Revolution: The End of Integration*

What signaled the fact that the civil rights movement was deepening into the Black Revolution was the end of integration as the goal of the struggle for ethnic liberation. Conversionism of only a slightly different kind than

Troeltsch spoke of died as this process took shape. The only thing wrong with Troeltsch's explorations into the plural world of historical individualities was that it could be dismissed as an intellectual game. But what he was attempting to explicate cannot be ignored in the context of America's ethnic pluralism, for this is concrete and indelible, tangible and visible. The trouble is that, whereas it has always been concrete, indelible, tangible, and visible, it has always been ignored. It cannot be ignored now.

The decisive issue forced into the open by the Black Revolution and all that it has generated is the issue of the interpretation of American history—an issue that integrationism consistently elided. A compelling case can be made for the view that this is the locus of the radical trauma for whites. It arrived with the sharp turn in what had been known as the civil rights movement. That movement may be characterized as the last-ditch effort by all concerned to find a way of simply incorporating into the mechanism of the American social-political-economic arrangement all who had hitherto been left out. That this arrangement was, and is, systemically racist was profoundly overlooked by the great majority of the participants in the movement, even including some of the minority leaders themselves. Immensely significant though they are, the phenomena of activism do not alone disclose where the real depths and causes of injustice are to be discerned. Blacks and reds may well struggle, vigorously and heroically, to become whites, with all the rights and privileges thereof, and *leave intact* the systemically racist arrangement itself. It is only when the violence done to history is faced that a perception of the real revolution springs to the fore. And it is only when history, with new agony and new insight, is given its due that truly revolutionary possibilities have a chance to flourish. This is an ancient lesson, as any careful investigation of the use of the Old Testament by the writers of the New Testament clearly indicates. But it is a lesson that is receiving a radically new reading in America today. The real revolutionaries begin their discipline pondering the true past. This is precisely where the significant thinkers in America's ethnic revolutions are to be found today.

No better exemplar of the issues now before us can be found than the brilliant black essayist Vincent Harding. Harding has been chairman of the Department of History at Spelman College, Atlanta; also director of the Martin Luther King, Jr., Center at the Interdenominational Theological Center in Atlanta; and director of the Institute of the Black World, also in Atlanta. His basic theme has been the call for "a new American history." Why a *new* American history? For Harding the answer is self-evident: "There will be no new beginnings for a nation that refuses to acknowledge its real past." [10]

Is there a way "beyond America's long dying"? [11] This memorable phrase comes from one of Harding's most significant essays, "Beyond Chaos: Black History and the Search for the New Land" (1970). His point of departure in this essay is his distinction between "Negro History" and "Black History." Of the many powerful articulations of the rise of the term "black" as the replacement for the term "Negro," which the events of these latter years have evoked, his is at once the most profound and the most illuminating. Harding sets the mood of his discussion as follows:

This essay is itself an attempt to come to terms with the fathers and to understand the nature of the new paths we younger black historians have begun to walk. As such it is a tentative set of suggestions, a brooding over the past and present in search of meaning, form, and possibly hope.[12]

What are these "new paths"? What is the shift involved? Harding does not deal with this lightly. He salutes the work of celebrated men such as George Washington Williams, Carter G. Woodson, John Hope Franklin, and Benjamin Quarles. But in so doing, he makes the case that a decisive turning point has been reached, one which had already been envisioned by Du Bois.[13] As over against the Negro historians' passion to demonstrate the role of blacks in the unfolding of the American dream, and thus to secure a place for at least some blacks in its fulfillment, black historians have reached a new sense of purpose:

> We cannot see luster when we must glimpse it through oceans of tears. We cannot—do not wish to—write with detachment from the agonies of our people. We are not satisfied to have our story accepted into the American saga. We deal in redefinitions, in taking over, in moving to set our own vision upon the blindness of American historiography.[14]

No better lines can be found to demonstrate our contention that real revolutionaries begin their discipline pondering the true past:

> Black History does not seek to highlight the outstanding contributions of special black people to the life and times of America. Rather our emphasis is on exposure, disclosure, on reinterpretation of the entire American past.[15]

Much is yet to come from the glowing intensity of the creativity of Vincent Harding. Even so it may well be that he has already crystallized one of the basic elements of his contribution. His decisive concern has to do not with the past alone but with the new future its reinterpretation entails. This is always the case when deep disputes take shape in historical analysis. The central component of Harding's radical reinterpretation of American history is his

insistence that the controlling interpretation of black experience in America must come from the hands of black
scholarship. His contention receives its most incisive expression in the controversy surrounding the widely read
novel by William Styron, *The Confessions of Nat Turner*.[16]
In the face of the general acclaim accorded this novel, an
extremely important work emerged under the title *William
Styron's Nat Turner: Ten Black Writers Respond*.[17] Harding's contribution to this symposium is entitled "You've
Taken My Nat and Gone." [18] Early in the fall of 1968,
Eugene D. Genovese's scathing review of the symposium,
with Harding as one of his principal targets, was published
in *The New York Review of Books*.[19] Harding's response
appeared later in the fall of 1968 in this same periodical
(along with two others, plus Genovese's response to the
responses, in which he utterly misses the point). It contains
a remarkable paragraph:

> In the essay I referred largely to that tragedy created by the
> non-black authorities on black life who are certain that they
> have eaten and drunk so fully of our experience that they are
> qualified to deliver homilies to us (at the least provocation)
> on how that experience should best be understood, recorded
> and lived, now and in the future. In essence they seek
> (perhaps unconsciously, but nonetheless effectively) to be-
> come the official keepers of our memories and the shapers of
> our dreams. I suggested that the society which eagerly
> accepts such assumptions offers to those of us who are black
> a slavery at once more subtle and more damaging than any
> we have known before.[20]

This should dispel once and for all any remaining
confusion as to why the white liberal is *the* enemy in the
eyes of the Black Revolution. Countless whites, many on
record, found themselves shaken and altered by the Styron
novel. They thought themselves new men and women as a

result of this. They thus misconstrued, as indeed the culture trains them to do, the staggering significance of the fact that Styron is white and a Southerner to boot. This was indeed the authenticating note in their eyes. "If a Southerner can see this much why can't I?" must, in some form, be on the heart of every alert white reader of Styron's attempt to do justice to the remarkable figure, Nat Turner. Such is, in effect, the ground taken by Genovese in his initial review, and in his response to the responses to it.

From the standpoint of black historians in particular, and of black revolutionaries in general, this is the precise locus of the real opposition. The assumption by white liberals that the impasse of the black/white crisis can be resolved by the formula of sincerity plus knowledge plus skill in articulation is the real barrier because it bespeaks *no genuine change*. This becomes clear only when the last bastion—the citadel of the shapers of dreams and the rulers of the future—is confronted. Willingness to accept a shared deliverance into a composite tomorrow, one which all must have a hand in shaping, is the only sure sign that this last redoubt has begun to collapse.

So it is that the deep purpose of Harding's labors takes shape around what he calls "the search for the new land, the new society, the new being." [21] Critical insights abound as he sketches the outlines of this search, and their telling effect moves in more than one direction. On the one hand, those who would reduce his vision simply to the liberation of blacks are challenged to understand that "blacks must read history with Indian eyes as well." [22] Only so can the real contradiction at the level of the origins of America as we know it be discerned.

Such a reading of America presses us to ask whether it was ever a democracy, demands to know whether it is possible for a democracy to exist where one quarter of the population of the land is either in slavery or being steadily driven off its ancient grounds. Black History is not simply "soul food" and "soul music" as some of its misinterpreters have suggested. Black History is the history of the Black Experience in America, which is the history of black and white—and Indian—inextricably, painfully, rarely joyfully, entwined.[23]

What if the inextricable entwining of red, white, and black could be the occasion of joy, rather than pain—joy because of the immense creative possibilities that the inexhaustible exchanges of such an irremovable diversity could generate? To hear Harding is to know this question. But to know this question is to know that the possibility of "integration" has disappeared once and for all. On the other hand, then, the most devastating of his indictments comes to the fore. Integration means the assimilation of reds and blacks (and all others, for that matter) into a white world that is doomed with the incurable disease of its own myopia. *Given the white world as it is, who would want to integrate with it?* Harding is not the first to press this question. His version of it, however, is unusually memorable, for it combines aggressive urgency with the cold wrath and impeccable cogency of knowledgeable reflection:

So Black History explores Henry Adams concerning the American nation at the beginning of the nineteenth century and hears him say that America in 1800 was a healthy organism. Then in the same work we read that the one major problem in America in 1800 was "the cancer" of slavery. In that set of statements America is diagnosed for black eyes: Healthy—except for cancer. . . . So, listening to the historian Henry Adams, [black historians] shape their own political question: Who wants to integrate with can-cer?[24]

New histories yield new identities. The rejection of "integration" as the term to describe the new land for which the oppressed seek is the necessary first step toward the realization of what this means. The Black Revolution had to be! For without the note of conflict the urgency of change diminishes, and the exhausting labor of the reinterpretation of the past in the name of a new tomorrow becomes optional, and then dies. But is that new tomorrow envisioned as a composite, and if so, can that composite be recognized on a theological ground? Thinking back to Troeltsch, now, the question can be put this way: Can the *historical individualities* that are the great ethnic identities *meet* in an open conversation about an ultimate liberation in which all share? The theological dimension is explicitly present in Harding's labors, and the same intensity informs it that we have already observed. His "The Religion of Black Power" [25] culminates with a trenchant shaping of the question of God-language, now so irrevocably a part of the theological enterprise, the question as to whether belief in the Ultimate in any sense is possible for anyone today. Unlike the usual ways in which this comes up, however, Harding's insights are forged directly out of the new identity his pursuit of Black History has disclosed:

> If racism rages as deep into American life as it appears and if violence is its closest brother, then a black revolution will no more solve the problem than a civil war did. . . . So it may be most responsible to ask if it is more than despair to speak of a long, grueling battle with no victory—and no illusions— this side of the grave? Has it been important and necessary simply to learn that there are no large citizen armies of white deliverers? Was it not absolutely necessary that all trust in courts and troops and presidents be shattered? Is this part of a black coming of age, a coming which will eventually reveal that even the black God of the ghetto is dead? [26]

Harding does more than formulate this question, and he does more than muse on it. He begins to point toward its resolution:

> Perhaps, though, he is not dead. Perhaps this new God has not lived long enough to die. Perhaps there is still a Beloved Community ahead. But if it is, it must be seen as the Kingdom whose realization does not depend upon whether whites (or anyone else around) really want it or not. If it comes, it may come only for the sake of its Lord, recognizing that even if He is black, the final glory is not the glory of blackness, but a setting straight of all the broken men and communities of the earth.[27]

Any struggle with ultimacy must sound a universal note, and Harding's is no exception. But in his thought this note is sounded in a way that does not destroy his identity by engulfing him in the torrents of an abstract concept of humanity-in-general. It is as a *black* thinker that he ponders these things—it is with black resources as well as the Christian tradition in its received form that he reflects:

> . . . Afro-Americans enter the experience that many people have known before them, people who in time of national crisis have turned to the gods they knew before the coming of Christian missionaries, seeking for what seemed a more solid ground. Nor should it be forgotten that such searches have taken place in this century no less significantly in Ireland and Germany than in Kenya and the Congo.[28]

And from this come two haunting questions. Both change and *the void* are present when a mind as creative and as free as Harding's is at work. "Can one accept the Yoruba dreams and dress without falling sway to its world view? Only the questions are available now." [29] His thought would be compelling enough if only this were seen! But the closing lines of the essay are even deeper. Is an apocalyptic resolution the only portent of the rise of Black Power?

Was it for this that we have come so painfully far together—
and yet apart—in this strange land? Was it only for this? Is
there no saving message from the drums of our homeland, or
did all gods die at once? [30]

No simple answer on the basis of theology as we now know
it can deal with these questions. A theology in red, white,
and black might begin to work with them. But we must
hear the red side of the triangle before we can begin to
suggest how this could be.

C. *The New Emergence of Red Dignity*

As we have already suggested, Du Bois was right in more
convoluted ways than he realized. The problem of the
twentieth century is not the problem of the color line, it is
the problem of the color *lines.* Events have demonstrated
this. What has begun as the Black Revolution cannot be
contained within the confines of the black/white crisis. Red
brothers and sisters have always known their own dignity,
but this dignity has taken its own stride toward freedom in
the context of the deepening of the civil rights movement.
Harding, as we have noted, is sensitive to this. What he
points to was receiving, even as he wrote, a vigorous and
forceful articulation at the hand of the astonishing Sioux
activist, Vine Deloria, Jr. Deloria is robustly forthright in
his return from Christianity to his own Sioux, or better,
Dakota, religious heritage. More than that, he is profoundly
informed to a degree that lends cogency to the intrinsic
power and clarity with which he writes. His great-grand-
father was a medicine man of the Yankton tribe of the Sioux
nation. His grandfather, a Yankton chief, converted to
Christianity and became a celebrated Episcopal priest. His
father, recently retired, culminated his career as the Episco-

pal Archdeacon of the Missionary District of South Dakota.[31] He himself took a B.D. at Augustana Theological Seminary (Lutheran), and then moved beyond this to earn a law degree at the University of Colorado. He is now preoccupied with the cause of tribal rights.[32] His writing moved from articles to books with the publication of his widely read *Custer Died for Your Sins* (1969) and *We Talk, You Listen* (1970). *Of Utmost Good Faith* (1971) followed, and then his fourth book, *God Is Red* (1973), certain to be accorded increasingly close attention, made its appearance.

The point with which we must begin demands great care, for it has to do with the tension between red and black, as well as that between red and white, and hence its exploration can well serve oppressors by informing their longstanding strategy of divide and conquer. The problem which cannot be avoided is this: The struggle for red liberation is *not* precisely analogous to the struggle for black liberation. This came into the open, once and for all, during the Poor People's March on Washington in the spring of 1968, and it was rooted in the planning for this effort.

> When [Martin Luther] King began to indiscriminately lump together as one all minority communities on the basis of their economic status, Indians became extremely suspicious. The real issue for Indians—tribal existence within the homeland reservation—appeared to have been completely ignored.[33]

More than the overlooking of decisive dynamics is involved in this problem. Deloria unmasks an utterly fallacious assumption:

> The whole of American society has been brainwashed into believing that if it understood blacks it could automatically understand every other group simply because blacks were the most prominent minority group with which white society had to deal.[34]

The devastating result of the operation of this assumption, *wherever* it functions, is that "the Indian is defined as a subcategory of black." [35] No group willingly accepts an external definition of itself, *wherever* it originates. We dare not leave the matter here, however. The issue is not that whites and blacks are equally oppressive of reds. The real polarity is rather that of *whites* vs. *blacks,* on the one hand, *whites-and-blacks-in-tension* vs. *reds,* on the other. The onus of generating the situation in which red is defined as a subcategory of black rests with those whose heritage is the defining of all other than themselves. Thus with Deloria, just as with Harding, the depth of the issue at hand has to do with the understanding of America's true past.

> The understanding of the racial question does not ultimately involve understanding by either blacks or Indians. It involves the white man himself. He must examine his past. He must face the problems he has created within himself and within others. The white man must no longer project his fears and insecurities onto other groups, races, and countries. Before the white man can relate to others he must forego the pleasure of defining them. The white man must learn to stop viewing history as a plot against himself.[36]

Deloria does not write as an American Indian, he writes as a Sioux. To grasp the significance of this remark is to enter the tribal world of the red brothers and sisters. "The Indians" exist as a monolithic entity only in white—and black—minds. This is not to say that there is no such thing as American Indians, but it is to say that there is no such thing as *the* American Indian. Red brothers and sisters know the heavy burden of stereotyping from all quarters, and that in a convoluted sense, for even when the decisive dimension of tribal identity is recognized by those from without it is almost invariably misunderstood.

If there is one single cause which has importance today for Indian people, it is tribalism. But creation of modern tribalism has been stifled by the ready acceptance of the "Indians-are-a-folk-people" premise of the anthropologists.[37]

The profound anger this distortion generates is most evident in a remark that may sound like a humorous aside, but which in actuality contains seething outrage, since it points to the fact of a continuous living affront that *all* Indians suffer at the hands of external generalizations. *All* the tribes are in trouble when the genius of each is casually denied.

The Sioux warbonnet, pride of the Plains Indians, became the universal symbol of Indianism. Even tribes that had never seen an eagle were required to wear a warbonnet to protect their lineage as Indians.[38]

This brings us to the real heart of Deloria's work, the effort to delineate the *present* reality of tribalism as over against the caricatures of the stereotypes. He warns his readers that his attempt is controversial both within and without the real world. "Tribalism," he insists, "can only be presented in mosaic form. . . . No single idea inevitably leads to another. The total impact of tribalism is thus not dependent upon acceptance of a single thesis." [39] The risk of even sounding like a spokesman for all the tribes is formidable indeed, and Deloria is perfectly aware of his vulnerability in this regard. Even so, it is a risk that must be run if either the pattern of oppression that *all* the tribes know, or the potential contributions that they can and must make, are to be recognized. For the prevailing fact of the tribal identity of all red brothers and sisters is the clue to both.

The decisive focus of the oppression that Indians know is the issue of broken treaties. More is at stake here than simply setting the record straight, though the shattering facts are clear: "America has yet to keep one Indian treaty or agreement despite the fact that the United States government signed over four hundred such treaties and agreements with Indian tribes." [40] The heart of the matter lies deeper. It is this: "The betrayal of treaty promises has in this generation created a greater feeling of unity among Indian people than any other subject." [41] Why is this the case? Deloria insists that the non-Indian world must understand that tribalism is nothing less than a way of grasping the totality of human existence.

> Culture, as Indian people understood it, was basically a life-style by which a people acted. It was a self-expression but not a conscious self-expression. Rather, it was an expression of the essence of a people.[42]

This bears heavily on the issue at hand, for it informs one of the most fundamental elements of the world of the red brothers and sisters, the *absolute integrity of the spoken word*.

> In an absolutely democratic social structure like the Indian tribe, formal legal negotiations and contractual arrangements were nearly out of the question. Once a man's word was given it bound him because of his integrity, not because of what he had written on a sheet of paper.[43]

Here it would seem clear that whereas Deloria's is a single voice, he is in fact speaking for all the tribes. The bill of particulars that all Indians hold against white America is staggering indeed. It unfolds the heritage of the broken word.

Is there a way beyond the dead end of the heritage of the broken word? Deloria is convinced that there is, and his articulation of this demonstrates what we mean in speaking of the new emergence of red dignity, for it is not only his profound grasp of his own tribal heritage that informs his suggestion; his own legal and theological training is also involved. He speaks not only as an interpreter of the past but as a participant in the present with a hope for a new tomorrow. As Deloria sees it, the impasse that has been reached in our time is that between minority people, who have no choice but to think and live as groups, and an entrenched white majority, which sublimates its own diversity of group origins in favor of a received tradition of individualism. The minority people yearn for genuine covenants that respect their group identities. The entrenched majority, however sincerely motivated and passionately committed to reversing ancient wrongs, responds with hopelessly individualistic programs for bringing aid to particular foci of suffering.[44] This is the setting within which Deloria proposes an impressive periodization of the history of American constitutional law. Two crises have come and gone; a third now impends:

[1]. The Civil War was fought to define the meaning of the word "men" in the Constitution.[45]

[2]. In a mere decade from 1954 to 1964 American society covered a century of time in defining what the word "citizen" meant. Then the civil rights movement shifted into group rights with the rise of Black Power.[46]

[3]. We are now in the midst of the third ideological American revolution. It is the struggle to define the phrase "we the people." [47]

Deloria's elaboration of this "third ideological American revolution" must be given close scrutiny. The theological dimension is explicit, as indeed it would have to be for an American Indian thinker. The tribal heritage is intrinsically and pervasively religious, and this fact must be taken into account in the resolving of this third crisis in the evolution of American constitutional law.

> The contemporary interpretation of "we the people" in reality means "we the peoples," we the definable groups, and thus admits minority groups into Constitutional protection which they should have received as groups a century ago. This is the first and vital step in thinking that must be made if we are to continue on as a society until we have developed and understood the basis upon which we can be a varied people, inhabiting one nation with laws that can be used to fulfill all expectations of the cultural, social, economic, and religious nature of man in his own group. To continue merely on the basis of an abstract individual contracting with other individuals would be to court disaster.[48]

Everything depends on the awareness of the fact that when Deloria speaks of the "religious nature of man in his own group" he is speaking with the passion of a genuine radical making anything but an innocuous observation. Precisely the religious nature of the American Indian in his own tribe has been, and continues to be, the central target of the missionary enterprise. The point to the Christian gospel has been that Indians must stop being Indians and become white men and women—such has been the impact of the good news on the tribes. In the light of Deloria's aggressive argument as a whole it becomes clear that from the beginning of its encounter with the red brothers and sisters, white Christianity has been misled by a profound double misunderstanding. Its passion was to approach "the Indian tribes in an effort to bring them into western European religious life." [49] This meant that it must seek to alter not the edges but the center of the totality of the life it found. Two oversimplifications became operational instantaneously: the hasty assumption that what was found had been the demonic, and the fallacious assumption that what was produced would be redemptive. These conspired to yield a tragically misconstrued confidence in results. It never occurred to white Christians, and too often it still does not, that the *de facto* results of their efforts could be *less*, not more, meaningful than what was replaced. What was, and is, faith for one man, could be, and can be, empty delusion for another. The same is true of people.

> Missionaries looked at the feats of the medicine men and proclaimed them to be works of the devil. They overlooked the fact that the medicine men were able to do marvelous things. Above all, they overlooked the fact that what the Indian medicine men did *worked*.
>
> Most activity centered on teaching and preaching. The thrust was to get the Indians to memorize the Large Catechism, the Small Catechism, the Apostles Creed, the Nicene Creed, the Ten Commandments, and other magic rites and formulas dear to Christianity. Salvation became a matter of regurgitation of creeds. In a very real sense, then, Christianity replaced living religions with magic.[50]

Thus new magic replaced old medicine, and the spirit and potential of red brothers and sisters was, and remains, under mortal assault.

It need not have been so, it must not remain so—witness the very creeds Deloria specifies! Christians long before had encountered cultures that at first they wrote off, only later to embrace, and thus to discover new insights into their own understanding of the Ultimate. But when they came to the shores of what for them was a "new world" they forgot this, and thus proclaimed the finality of their own conclusions, refusing in advance the possibility of yet another refinement of their own attempt to serve their Lord.

Deloria knows, probably as well as, if not better than, any American Indian thinker today, that a specifically Indian understanding of the Christian faith has always been a genuine, though continually thwarted, possibility. He also knows what has blocked it.

> I believe that an Indian version of Christianity could do much for our society. But there is little chance for such a melding of cards. Everyone in the religious sphere wants his trump to play on the last trick.[51]

In the context of ethnic pluralism no one has a monopoly on the last trick—not Deloria, not Harding, not Troeltsch! One thing only is clear: the issues raised by each of them must receive a treatment that none has yet received in a theology in red, white, and black.

D. *The Discipline*

The initial step toward a theology in red, white, and black is the step of listening. Each side of the triangle must be heard. This listening must be rigorously disciplined, for only so will what one expected to hear be replaced by the recognition of what the other two are in fact saying. The promising yield of disciplined diversity is the deepening of new questions, forged by unexpected exchange, and demanding unprecedented reflection. Two qualities characterize the discipline of life-in-diversity: *expectancy* and *waiting*.

First, then, the quality of *expectancy*—the expectancy of the new disclosure, the anticipation of new aspects of the reality of each of the others, which one can know only if the others are understood. The discipline of expectancy must be practiced by *all* who would reach the plane of mutual intelligibility. And it *is* a matter of discipline, for it demands the conscious efforts of all who would move "beyond America's long dying." [52]

Conscious effort, on the part of all—red, white, and black? Why? What is involved is a dimension of reality that ought to be, but is not, self-evident. The fact that it is not self-evident is a major clue to the pervasiveness of the racism that has distorted all three sides of the red/white/black triangle. When *historical individualities* do reach the plane of mutual intelligibility, prior stereotypes emerge as ludicrous guesses as to what each had thought, hoped, dreamed, and dared. This is why persistent effort of the most rigorous kind is necessary in order to inhabit this plane. In a word, it is hard to admit the incongruity of the distortions one formerly thought were truths. It is hard because resistance to the unanticipated lies deeply embedded under layers of cultural conditioning, where incongruous distortions masquerade both as profound compassion and as unrequitable outrage. Those who think they have admitted the necessity of mutual intelligibility will find their certainty tested at the moment when they discover that the reality of the others is not what they had assumed it to be.

To know and to celebrate life in diversity takes the effort of eager expectancy. This effort is informed and strengthened by the knowledge that *no* historical individuality is a subcategory of any other. It is indeed one of the most far-reaching and priceless insights to have been confirmed by the turbulent years of ethnic revolutions.

Secondly, the quality of *waiting.* The development of mutual intelligibility across the lines separating historical individualities is a slow business. Old assumptions must give way before newly recognized clarities, and a new vocabulary of exchange, stripped of the passion of ideological imperialism, must unfold. This takes time even when the self-conscious identities of the historical individualities in question are hoary with informing traditions. When, however, the self-conscious identities of a set of historical individualities are *new*, when both traditions and the understanding of them receive the stimulus of radical changes of direction and abrupt shifts in perspective, the urgency of the discipline of waiting is intensified a thousandfold. This is precisely the case with the new emergence of the dignity of identity that America's ethnic revolutions have generated. The astonishing fact is that *new* historical identities are shaping, and the lingering effect of the history of ethnic oppression is evident in the fact that they must fight for time to develop.

Of all the failings of whites who themselves struggle to grasp their own new sense of identity in the context of celebrated diversity none is worse than their failure to practice the regimen of waiting. Nothing so obstructs the emergence of genuine mutual intelligibility as the compulsion to speed a process whose dynamics and tempo are not susceptible to external control. It is easy to understand this passion for haste; guilt is always anxious for absolution. But the passion for haste fails to recognize the amount of time that is required for new thought to arise, develop, know testing in the crucible of knowledgeable debate, and then flourish.

To say this raises the grim specter of gradualism, the epithet always flung by those whose patience is exhausted by the world of hostility that is now normative. Waiting in the service of mutual intelligibility is not to be confused with waiting as the tactic of the enemies of change. Waiting, in the context of celebrated diversity, in the service of the eager expectancy of new disclosures, is itself a creative, not destructive, and an active, not passive, effort.

It is the waiting of a participant, not the waiting of a spectator. It is, above all, the waiting of the changing, not the delay of the reluctant. It is the waiting evoked by respect for the others. It is disciplined waiting—disciplined in the presence of the dignity of new identities.

The discipline of mutual intelligibility, comprised of expectancy and waiting, points the way toward the realization of a theology in red, white, and black. If just the taking of this initial step became widespread, much would be accomplished. For now we can begin to see with a sense of clarity what was only a dim, far horizon for Troeltsch fifty years ago. We can see that conversionism must come to an end. The inhabitants of the ethnically plural world know that they can *never* become each other. They know that the changes that must occur if America is to move beyond its long dying are changes that must be shared as the pluralism itself comes to know its diversity as the condition of joy. They know that the new gospel must combine with old medicine if the liberation of that old search is to experience expansion into an even broader, even deeper, recognition of the Ultimate. Theology in red, white, and black must move beyond all attempts of any kind whatsoever that seek to render any single historical individuality as the master of all others.

It is striking, in this light, to reflect on the fact that *conversion* and *integration* are close cousins, maybe even twin brothers! They share a common fallacious assumption, the assumption that ultimacy will best be served only if all are alike. The discipline of mutual intelligibility arises from precisely the opposite conviction, that ultimacy is recognizable only when differences are understood and cherished. Could it be that there is an astonishing latency in one of Jesus' sayings: "Where two or three are gathered in my name, there am I in the midst of them" (Matt. 18:20)? We have always assumed that "in my name" limits "two or three." Could it be that only "two or three" can give meaning to "in my name"? More must be seen before we can reckon fully with the depths of this risky reversal. But one thing is already clear: It can be dismissed, quickly and quietly, only by those who listen to the new disclosures of rising identities not in order to relate, but in order to conquer.

3:

THE PROMISE
OF MUTUAL INTERDEPENDENCE

THE DISCIPLINE OF MUTUAL INTELLIGIBILITY IS NOT
enough, in and of itself, to yield a theology in red, white,
and black. The change entailed is too deep. Disciplined
effort alone cannot effect it. Accompanying and informing
this discipline there must be a sense of vision, a sense of
purpose. The incentive to living under the discipline of
mutual intelligibility has to do with the promise of mutual
interdependence. But this forces into the open critical
considerations that cannot be avoided if this promise is
taken seriously. What can happen if one listens in order not
to conquer, but to relate? What does the new relationship
portend? What does it exclude?

At this stage of our discussion we shall confine our direct
attention to the black/white exchange, just as in the next
chapter we shall develop the points at hand in red/white
terms. This is necessary because the material before us
must be pondered in detail. In each instance, though, it will
become clear that as the perception of these theological
issues deepens, the implications that begin to take shape
both can and must be applied to the red/white/black
triangle as a whole, and ultimately, to the full mosaic that is
humanity.

A. *The Gospel and the Basic Form of Humanity*

The I-Thou principle is virtually a commonplace for anyone working in the realm of theology today. What is not as generally recognized as it ought to be is that if this insight is taken seriously it is of revolutionary significance. To begin at the beginning on the matter is to take up a central element of the thought of Martin Buber. I-Thou and I-It are "primary words," as Buber put it.[1] The virtually inexhaustible point is that there is a radical distinction between the "I" in I-Thou and the "I" in I-It. To recognize the other as a Thou, a person rather than a thing, is to know a fundamental shift in one's own sense of identity, which forever binds one to the world of other Thou-recognizing "I's." The variations on this profound theme so memorably enunciated by Buber are legion. The most significant of them for us is the version worked out by Karl Barth, for it drove him to an explication of what he called "The Basic Form of Humanity," [2] and his full articulation of this is pivotal, not only for his understanding of the claim of the gospel, but also for our understanding of what is at stake for theology in the context of ethnic pluralism.

It will always be difficult to touch Barth lightly. His thought found its lasting expression in the monumental *Church Dogmatics*, with its layers-upon-layers of convoluted theological argument, all of it serving his basic theme that Christology must explicitly pervade the entire range of Christian doctrinal reflection. Complicated though his way of saying this is, however, it is precisely for this reason that the trail he blazed, and not that charted by Buber, is the one we must be aware of in our own discussion. For despite his many theological opponents, Barth did indeed have a robust doctrine of humanity, one that is intimately tied to his Christological doctrine of God. This reflected the depths of his involvement in the tempestuous decades of the 1930's and 1940's, and the struggle against the Third Reich, and no understanding of his efforts as a whole can be valid if it does not reckon with the immediate context within which he worked. It should come as no surprise, then, that when his insight is exposed to the ferment of America's ethnic revolutions its far-reaching significance is more drastic than even he realized. For if he was correct, the issue cannot be stated too emphatically: If the basic form of humanity is in trouble, the gospel is in jeopardy. Barth knew this to be so in the context of the German nightmare. We must know what it implies in the context of America's struggle to transcend *its* long dying.

Barth grounded his discussion of "The Basic Form of Humanity" in his elaboration of the I-Thou principle. Arguing that humanity may not be understood individualistically, he insisted that the phrase "I am" must be taken to mean "I am in encounter," which he then refined immediately to read "I am as Thou art." [3] His explication of this basic formula moved through four steps: (1) Being in encounter means that "one looks the other in the eye"— they meet.[4] (2) Being in encounter means that having met, they "speak to each other, and hear each other." [5] His elaboration of this step is fourfold. As he put it: "Humanity as encounter must become the event of speech. And speech comprehensively means: mutual expression and the mutual perception of it, mutual address and the mutual perception of it. None of the four elements may be missing." [6] Thus both in its initial (and therefore superficial) sense, and in its lasting (and therefore deep) sense, the speech event must be shared in genuine, reciprocating fashion. (3) Being in encounter means that "in the act of being" each gives to the other "mutual help." [7] No one can be himself or herself alone. (4) Finally, Barth insisted that the entire "happening" of the basic form of humanity "stands under the sign that it happens, from both sides, *gladly* [*gerne*]." [8] That Barth could build his major point on an adverb points to his theological virtuosity. Putting the matter as he did, he was able to insist that the opposite of "gladly" is not simply "unwillingly" but "neutrally." This was his version of the whole I-Thou business, namely, that cynicism is the real enemy of human existence, and that therefore mutuality is its true opposite.

Now the question is, how far did Barth mean to take this final opposition of "gladly" vs. "neutrally"? And how far must we push it? In his own way, Barth was willing to take it to the ultimate reaches, insisting that nothing less than the thrust of the gospel itself is at stake, and since the matter defies simple formulation he devoted a long note to its analysis. The point to this note is that for Barth this fourth step must pervade and inform the first three. [9] The fourth step provides the qualitative integrity of the I-Thou relationship that constitutes the basic form of humanity. As such, however, it does not constitute the content of Christian love, and this is the issue Barth sought to clarify in his long aside. The distinction in question is hardly of minimal significance, because if Barth was correct in his way of understanding it, then the proclamation of the gospel is tied to the championing of the highest potentialities of human creativity, those that can flourish only in the realm of the *gladly*, so to speak. We must follow the logic of this excursus, at least briefly, in order to see how this conclusion is, surprisingly, in order—*surprisingly* in order, since the stereotype has it that Barth never argued as he explicitly did here, and that we cannot hear him as we must hear him now.

Calvinists (though not Calvin) throughout four centuries —and surely Barth is the Calvinist *par excellence* in this century—have often been guilty of the most devastating minimizing of human nature in the attempt to maximize the understanding of the love and the grace of God. At the outset of the note Barth categorically rejected this tendency.[10] It fails to understand that neither the alienating fact of sin, nor the even more astonishing fact of the love and grace of God, is implicit in the basic form of humanity. In Barth's system *each* of these is intelligible only in the light of God's self-revelation in Jesus Christ. Since this is the case it is *theologically* an error of the first magnitude even to insinuate that either sin or grace can be disclosed by probing the basic form of humanity. For this is to fail to recognize that the basic form of humanity stands in its own right. It is there for all to see, Christian and non-Christian alike (Barth mentioned Confucius, Feuerbach, and Buber as examples).[11] In the name of the uniqueness of the gospel, then, Barth may be seen as insisting on what could be called *the visible integrity of the basic form of humanity.* To be sure, he took a defensive posture in this insistence, for he wished to counter any equating of this visible integrity with the integrity of the gospel itself.

More was involved, however, than simply this defensive maneuver, significant though it is, for Barth's concern was not merely tactical in nature. The note culminated with his attempt to deal with a prevalent condition within Protestant thought, one that, ironically enough, he himself had helped to bring about (though he would have been the first to deny it). This was, and in some quarters remains, the championing of Hebraic thought at the expense of damning everything the marvelous world of ancient Greek reflection had to offer. There is, of course, a difference between these two realms of thought, and its delineation is crucial for theology, epitomized in the sharp contrast between *agape* and *eros*. But, warned Barth, "the Greeks with their *eros*

. . . comprehended that the essence of the human is that it is free, basically open, willing, spontaneous, joyful, cheerful, and social." [12] No reading of the gospel that suggests the contrary can be either helpful or compelling. This led Barth to a critical formulation, one whose significance both depends upon, and yet runs far beyond, his own system.

> But we know—and on this depended and depends every legitimate relationship between Christianity and Hellenism —that while we have gained our concept of humanity elsewhere, namely from the one, unique, real fact of salvation, the revelation of God, yet we cannot help but acknowledge that it finds in Greek man with his *eros* a confirmation, of which we have to think, and on which we have every reason to orient ourselves, when it is a matter of understanding Christian love as the awakening and fulfilling of humanity, of the distorted [*verkehrten*] and ruined [*verderbten*] but not lost [*verlorenen*] manner of the mutual man, that is, man as created by God.[13]

Now it should be clear that Barth was *not* saying that the uniqueness of the gospel is dependent upon the explication of the basic form of humanity. Barth never could, and never did, equate wisdom with faith. Even so, equally clearly, he was insisting on the fact that the uniqueness of the gospel must find *confirmations* in wisdom regarding the basic form of humanity when the issue is that of showing the relationship between Christian love and the fulfillment of humanity. In this sense the gospel is tied to the fact that being in encounter happens authentically only when it happens *gladly*. Many of Barth's doctrinaire followers saw, and will continue to see, only the first of these implications. But in the context of the ethnic revolutions we must see both of them.

The basic form of humanity stands in its own right. Its awakening and fulfillment is the point to the gospel. Its denial, for any reason, can only result in the most tragic of all happenings, the muting of the gospel itself so that it cannot be heard. Accordingly, the gospel is so intimately tied to the basic form of humanity that it dies when the latter is either crushed or ignored. A neutral gospel is no gospel at all—a lesson Barth labored endlessly to grasp and convey.

Both the contours of ruin and distortion, and the possibilities of awakening and fulfillment, stand out in sharp focus when the reality of ethnically plural humanity is embraced and celebrated—gladly. The promise of mutual interdependence contains each of these dimensions. Hidden in this promise are the individual's understanding of his or her fellow human, and the response of each to the God of them both. In order to see this, we must now ponder what Barth could not have known as we now must know; we must know, from the inside out, the relation between oppressed and oppressor. When we do, we shall be driven far beyond Barth along the path he so memorably discerned.

B. *The Oppressed as Teacher*

In the context of America's ethnic revolutions a new note has entered the range of the I-Thou spectrum. It is one thing to contemplate the radical fact that humanity is relational, through and through, and that accordingly individualism in any sense of the term is a total cul-de-sac. To take the other seriously, and to do so gladly—as we must always put it on this side of Barth's labors—reconstitutes the I. The role of the spectator is ruled out, the role of the participant is the only option. But what happens when this insight is jolted by the facts of racial oppression, against which the oppressed struggle, and which they have truly

unmasked? One can concede immediately that the whole
I-Thou business is intensified. But mere concession is not
enough. For to reflect on this matter is to encounter what
for many is a shocking disclosure, surely anything but
self-evident. The fact is that in the I-Thou relationship
between oppressed and oppressor an unevenness or imbalance comes to the fore. The weighted side of this imbalance
is *not* where the dominating majority (even the concerned
among them) and perhaps some of the dominated minorities
(including even the profound among them) might well
assume it to be. For the upper hand is that of the
oppressed, not the oppressor! Only when this is grasped
will the I-Thou concept become what it has always
struggled to be, not a containable insight, but a revolutionary principle.

The events of these recent years have forced any
American reflection on the I-Thou concept into extremely
radical channels. In this context it is the basic form of
humanity that is in trouble, simply because it continues to
be distorted by the tension between the oppressor and the
oppressed. Being in encounter cannot happen gladly when
oppression blocks the realization of the I-Thou possibility.
The upheavals that shake our time revolve around this
central issue, and *any* theology that ignores this is doomed
to serve only oppressors. There is a profound reason why, in
the context of the continuum of oppression, the oppressed
must take the lead in any effort to realize the I-Thou world.
For them, oppression is not an abstraction, it is the concrete
reality in the midst of which all life and thought unfold.
Only the oppressed can expose the reality of oppression.
Oppressors always want the term "oppression" to be kept at
the level of a controllable metaphor. There may be wisdom
to be found in so doing, but when the insights of the
oppressed are truly perceived, this wisdom will be seen to

be *derivative* in character. Once this is grasped, the possibility of new, mutual, reciprocating exchanges, each dependent on the other, arises—but it can do so *only* along the route of an oscillating exchange that begins from the side of the oppressed. This is one way to understand the lasting yield of the life and labors of Martin Luther King, Jr. Despite his detractors, he was the figure who—more than any other—began to teach America a lesson it did not wish to learn.

We have now lived long enough with the shattering pain of the assassination of Martin King so that there is little need for new attempts at the tribute that defies words. The noble grandeur of his martyrdom assures his place in the soul of America. The only tribute now in order is that of coming to terms with his lasting contribution. The mere mention of his name will always bring up the term "nonviolence," and this complicates the task at hand. Oppressors love nonviolence, for it provides them with time and room to find ways of keeping things as they are. For this very reason the oppressed are at least suspicious of it, if they do not reject it entirely. In either case, King's lasting contribution is either overlooked or ignored, for while it emerged along the path of his charismatic, prophetic spokesmanship it was nevertheless comprised of carefully considered theological components that can be discerned only by equally careful analysis. The demonic apathy of oppressors and the aggravated impatience of the oppressed inhibit such analysis.

King's understanding of nonviolence was always aggressive, a fact that was intensified by the culminating involvements of his life, especially the debate with his own black brothers over the rise of "Black Power." King's version of this debate is set out in detail in his last book, *Where Do We Go from Here: Chaos or Community?* (1968). To see the implications of his position in the crucible of this debate we must consider at least two of the decisive influences on his thought, Mohandas Gandhi and Reinhold Niebuhr. These influences are treated in his first book written ten years earlier, *Stride Toward Freedom: The Montgomery Story* (1958).[14]

The impact of Gandhi's thought on King was profound and permanent. What happened was that in his study of Gandhi he found the way to make Jesus' love ethic operational as a force for social change. The key moment in initiating this development that was to have such massive consequences occurred while King was a student at Crozer Theological Seminary. A lecture by Mordecai Johnson, president of Howard University, aroused his interest precisely at the time when his study of Nietzsche had virtually obliterated his faith in the power of love for the solving of social problems.[15] The study of Gandhi reversed this despair dramatically. "Prior to reading Gandhi," he tells us, "I had about concluded that the ethics of Jesus were only effective in individual relationships. . . . But after reading Gandhi, I saw how utterly mistaken I was."[16]

Decisive in King's grasp of Gandhi's case for nonviolence was the basic insight that it is an option only for the strong: "This is why Gandhi often said that if cowardice is the only alternative to violence, it is better to fight."[17] The point to nonviolence is not resignation, it is resistance. Inevitably, it will know suffering at the hands of powerful injustice, but this brings to the surface the conviction that "unearned suffering is redemptive."[18] King, of course, would understand this insight as a Christian, but it was Gandhi who showed him how. When the strong opt for nonviolence on this ground, the fundamental attitude toward their opponents is informed not by the vindictive effort to humiliate them, but by the passion to win them to the cause of a new humanity. This evoked an insight that King would never desert: "The aftermath of nonviolence is the creation of the beloved community, while the aftermath of violence is tragic bitterness." [19] For this beloved community to be realized nonviolence must be internalized into a way of life lest the enemy be hated, with the result that his evil would be reduplicated rather than overcome. Supporting such a vision is an abiding conviction that "the universe is on the side of justice," and that "the believer in nonviolence" is one who knows "that in his struggle for justice he has cosmic companionship." [20]

So understood, King's version of the case for nonviolence knew the gathering triumphs of Montgomery, Birmingham, and Selma, Alabama, and the shattering reverses of Athens, Georgia, and Chicago, Illinois. More than that, it knew the withering fire of invective and rejection in the debate with his brothers in the struggle, a debate in full process and anything but resolved when he was cut down by the assassin in Memphis, Tennessee. It is doubtful whether his conviction could have survived this debate had it been informed by the formula "Jesus plus Gandhi" alone. The fact that he had also been touched by Reinhold Niebuhr achieved its real significance only when his back was to the wall, not simply in the struggle against white injustice, but at the point when there was added to this the pressure of his brothers' unmasking of what threatened to deteriorate into noble naïveté.

It is one of those far-reaching accidents of history that King read Niebuhr after he had studied Gandhi. At first he was overwhelmed, finding Niebuhr so compelling that he nearly accepted his social ethics without reservation. The trouble was that King knew Gandhi, and thus he could not accept Niebuhr's appraisal of pacifism as being a combination of passive nonresistance with a simple trust in the power of love. Neither of these components may be present in any authentic *resistance* to evil. The issue for King as over against Niebuhr was caught up in precisely the notes of the aggressiveness and the purpose of nonviolence.

> True pacifism is not unrealistic submission to evil power, as Niebuhr contends. It is rather a courageous confrontation of evil by the power of love, in the faith that it is better to be the recipient of violence than the inflicter of it, since the latter only multiplies the existence of violence and bitterness in the universe, while the former may develop a sense of shame in the opponent and thereby bring about a transformation and change of heart.[21]

Niebuhr, though, left his mark on King, as he has on all who have worked carefully with his thought. It was one thing to call Niebuhr to task regarding pacifism. It was quite another to recognize that his argument as a whole obliterated false optimism. King admitted the cogency of Niebuhr's "extraordinary insight into human nature, especially the behavior of nations and social groups," and his "persistent reminder of the reality of sin on every level of man's existence." Thus,

> While I still believed in man's potential for good, Niebuhr made me realize his potential for evil as well. Moreover, Niebuhr helped me to recognize the complexity of man's social involvement and the glaring reality of collective evil.[22]

Ten years after writing these words (in *Stride Toward Freedom*) King would be forced to know and to argue a depth of understanding of this Niebuhrian perspective that he simply had not yet reached in the days of his rising influence after Montgomery. He hardly needed to be informed by Niebuhr as regards the reality of collective evil. No black person does! But he found himself compelled to comprehend the full range of the complexity of the social involvement of humanity in the face of those who shared his dream but rejected his case for nonviolent resistance. This was the context both of his last book, and of his lasting contribution, which took the shape of a decisive question that arose as the civil rights movement was deepening into the Black Revolution. That question formed the title of his last book, the attempt to answer it, its content.

The final refinement of King's thought grew out of the crisis, in the summer of 1966, surrounding James Meredith's Freedom March through Mississippi. King and key members of the staff of his Southern Christian Leadership Conference rallied to the scene when Meredith was wounded at the outset of the march, as did other black leaders of national stature, most significantly Stokely Carmichael of the Student Nonviolent Coordinating Committee, and Floyd McKissick of the Congress of Racial Equality. Questions that had long been smoldering now burst into the open with overwhelming force. What if the hope on which nonviolence is predicated is countered by no results? What if the opponent does not respond? What if nonviolent resistance, simply because it is nonviolent, evokes not change, but apathy at best, or obstruction at worst? In the face of the now unrequitable urgency of such questions King's leadership role in the cause of justice for black America was exposed to more severe strain than it had ever known before.[23]

As King looked back on the rise of the demand for Black Power he stated concisely and eloquently his basic concurrence with what he regarded to be its positive points, namely, its "cry of disappointment," [24] its demand for "political and economic strength" oriented toward the "legitimate goals" of a people,[25] and its "call to manhood." [26] He also formulated his critique of it, and in the process clarified and deepened his case for nonviolence as the only promising route to effective change. Two dimensions of this critique must be noted carefully.

In the first place, King argued against the despair he assumed to be present in the advocates of Black Power, a despair he regarded as rooted in "a nihilistic philosophy born out of the conviction that the Negro can't win." [27] He insisted that this fails to recognize that "Today's despair is a poor chisel to carve out tomorrow's justice." [28] Subsequent developments have shown that King was wrong in the appraisal. His observation that despair is not creative is cogent enough, but the Black Power movement was neither as nihilistic nor as devoid of constructive capacities as he thought it was. However that may be, King's struggle at this point was in the name of a realistic reading of the American scene, and in this respect he was, and remains, incisively correct.

> The American Negro will be living tomorrow with the very people against whom he is struggling today. The American Negro is not in a Congo where the Belgians will go back to Belgium after the battle is over, or in an India where the British will go back to England after independence is won. In the struggle for national independence one can talk about liberation now and integration later, but in the struggle for racial justice in a multiracial society where the oppressor and the oppressed are both "at home," liberation must come through integration.[29]

As we have seen, integrationism has died, and in a moment we shall see that King himself began to realize that the term was too tame to describe the new reality his efforts envisioned. The fact remains, however, that in this passage his statement of the problem could not have been more accurately formulated.

In the second place, this same sense of realism, evoked by

the debate with the advocates of Black Power, infused King's case for nonviolence with an even greater vigor than it had known before. The passage just cited already intimates this. Oppressors, by definition, resist any celebration of the multiracial character of society. They cannot be "at home" in a multiracial world. King now found himself unequivocally championing nonviolence, not as the most feasible way of achieving the assimilation of blacks into a white world, but as the necessary means of forcing change through the constructive use of tension. Whereas he rejected the violence of the Black Power cry, he asserted the *coercive* dimension of nonviolent resistance to the forces of racial injustice. This yielded both a conclusion and a sharply worded warning to the white community.

> The white liberal must rid himself of the notion that there can be a tensionless transition from the old order of injustice to the new order of justice. Two things are clear to me, and I hope they are clear to white liberals. One is that the Negro cannot achieve emancipation through violent rebellion. The other is that the Negro cannot achieve emancipation by passively waiting for the white race voluntarily to grant it to him. The Negro has not gained a single right in America without persistent pressure and agitation. . . . Society needs nonviolent gadflies to bring its tensions into the open and force its citizens to confront the ugliness of their prejudices and the tragedy of their racism.[30]

Both his persistence in proclaiming the cause of nonviolent resistance to evil and his embracing of the coercive weapon which this way of life possesses combined to inform King's final strategies and insights. In November and December of 1967, on this side of the debates set down in *Where Do We Go from Here . . . ?* and within six months of his death, King delivered the "Massey Lectures" for the Canadian Broadcasting Company, which were later published under the title, *The Trumpet of Conscience* (Harper & Row, Publishers, Inc., 1968). Now he served notice that nonviolence would be played henceforth in a new key: "I intend to show that nonviolence will be effective, but not until it has achieved the massive dimensions, the disciplined planning, and the intense commitment of a sustained, direct-action movement of civil disobedience on the national scale." [31] This accounts for both his announced stand against the war in Southeast Asia in the spring of 1967 [32] and the planning for the Poor People's March on Washington, which he did not live to see.

It accounts for even more. The escalation of the gospel of nonviolence to the level of massive, national civil disobedience generated the new note of realistic forcefulness present in King's culminating formulations of his longstanding conviction. This is remarkably evident in the development of one of his most memorable statements, but it can be seen only by way of close attention to detail. Toward the end of *Stride Toward Freedom*, in 1958, King worked out a moving paraphrase of Gandhi in order to bring Gandhi's witness directly to bear on the impasse faced by black America. The fifth and final element of the "Massey Lectures" was his sermon for Christmas Eve, 1967, at the Ebenezer Baptist Church in Atlanta, where he shared the pastorate with his father. Now he repeated, in slightly expanded form, this same paraphrase. The differences are those of nuance, but they are of great significance, for they demonstrate the deepening cogency of his conviction. The King that both was and is impugned is the King without these shifts. With them, he cannot be casually or caustically dismissed. The 1967 statement follows, with italics marking the additions:

> We shall match your capacity to inflict suffering by our capacity to endure suffering. We will meet your physical

force with soul force. Do to us what you will and we will still love you. We cannot in all good conscience obey your unjust laws *and abide by the unjust system, because noncooperation with evil is as much a moral obligation as is cooperation with good, and so throw us in jail and we will still love you.* Bomb our homes and threaten our children, and, as difficult as it is, we will still love you. Send your hooded perpetrators of violence into our communities at the midnight hour and drag us out on some wayside road and leave us half-dead as you beat us, and we will still love you. *Send your propaganda agents around the country, and make it appear that we are not fit, culturally and otherwise, for integration, and we'll still love you.* But *be assured that* we'll wear you down by our capacity to suffer, and *one day* we will win our freedom. *We will not only win freedom for ourselves;* we will so appeal to your heart and conscience that we will win you in the process, *and our victory will be a double victory.*[33]

Read without the italicized passages the paraphrase is basically the equivalent of the 1958 statement. There are other, extremely minor, editorial changes that need not be noted. But there is one decisive shift which the simple convention of italicizing additions cannot capture. The last two sentences no longer contain the word "soon." What King said in 1958 was: "But we will soon wear you down by our capacity to suffer. And in winning our freedom we will so appeal to your heart and conscience that we will win you in the process." [34] What he said in 1967 is given above. Epitomizing this facet of King's last paraphrase of Gandhi, then, we would have to say: "One day a double victory will be at hand. Our suffering will have won both our freedom, and yours." Gandhi alone stood behind the 1958 paraphrase. Gandhi, plus Niebuhr, plus King's own genius and a decade of convoluted struggles, stood behind the 1967 paraphrase.

Where do we go from here? Martin King gave his life to the tortuous refinement of this question, and it will live forever as the insistent urging toward a new, different tomorrow for all who would be taught by him. He had asked the question early, using it as the title for the closing chapter of his first book. The answer then was clear, though he could not have known its full portent: "Today the choice is no longer between violence and nonviolence. It is either nonviolence or nonexistence." [35] He asked it again at the close of his labors, the question now being the title of his last book. The subtitle, *Chaos or Community?* however, indicates only partially his last refinement of the decisive issue before the America of the closing decades of the twentieth century. The book ends with these words:

> We are now faced with the fact that tomorrow is today. We are confronted with the fierce urgency of *now*. In this unfolding conundrum of life and history there is such a thing as being too late. Procrastination is still the thief of time. Life often leaves us standing bare, naked and dejected with a lost opportunity. The "tide in the affairs of men" does not remain at the flood; it ebbs. We may cry out desperately for time to pause in her passage, but time is deaf to every plea and rushes on. Over the bleached bones and jumbled residues of numerous civilizations are written the pathetic words: "Too late." . . . We still have a choice today: nonviolent coexistence or violent coannihilation. This may well be mankind's last chance to choose between chaos and community.[36]

The vigorous optimism of the statement of the issue in 1958 was informed by the initial triumphs of Montgomery. Trial and testing lay ahead, as King no doubt knew full well, but these were faced with the certainty of an inevitable victory. The statement of the issue in 1967 likewise contained vibrant conviction, but King now knew that the effort could fail. He also knew how it could fail, and what the grim portent of such a collapse would entail. The accent now was not on the inevitability of triumph, but on the urgency of winning a cause that could be lost. And in the language that dominates his parting words that cause is not the cause of the peaceful integration of blacks into a white world, but of the nonviolent coexistence of each in a multiracial society.

King's is not the only voice to which we may listen. We did not begin with him, and later voices that we have heard, or have yet to hear, move even deeper than he did, incisive though he was. Even so, with something of his thought before us, the effect he had on the years given him becomes understandable, and the implications of his labors for a theology that seeks to take ethnic pluralism seriously emerge with unavoidable clarity. Whether he ultimately would have come to emphasize the idea of nonviolent coexistence in a multiracial society as we must now read it, in a time which, as we have seen, has come to know the end of integrationism, is a question that can never be resolved with finality. One thing is beyond debate, however. For those with ears to hear King began the process of teaching an unexpected lesson. The liberation of oppressed *and* oppressor begins with the struggle of the oppressed against oppression. This is not merely an unexpected lesson, it is a lesson that *only* the oppressed can teach, for only the oppressed can reveal to the oppressor that the removal of oppression is not an option but an absolute necessity. Only the oppressed, by their insistence, can deliver the oppressors from the demonic assumption that the removal of oppression is an option. Both oppressed and oppressor share this liberation. They are dependent upon each other for the final breaking of the impasse that oppression causes and perpetuates. King put this in a way that can be fatally ignored by oppressed and oppressor alike, but, given his final insights, it is a true clue to a radical transformation: "Negroes hold only one key to the double lock of peaceful change. The other is in the hands of the white community." [37] Which white community? The white community that has been forced to recognize itself as the source of oppression; has become dependent upon the insight of oppressed blacks into the absolute necessity of change; and thus has become linked with them in the struggle for this change, which might be optimal if peacefully wrought.

The farthest reach of the lesson taught by King thus comes into view. The simple proclamation of the gospel of reconciliation was not enough to effect the needed liberation. The focus of this need is at the point of the basic form of humanity. Being in encounter can never happen authentically—gladly!—when oppression blocks the fulfillment of the I-Thou dream. Both the distortion and ruin and the awakening and fulfillment of the multiracial society turn on this fact. The distortion and ruin of multiracial humanity will culminate in violent coannihilation if King's warning to all involved is ignored. The awakening and fulfillment of multiracial humanity correlates with this, for however it is construed, whether at the hands of the gospel of Jesus the Christ, or at the hands of any other attempt to realize ultimate worth and dignity, it must either await or accompany the removal of oppression. For King, whose passion was indeed rooted in the gospel, this meant that Christian conviction must be joined to and informed by massive civil disobedience on a national scale, for only in the context of this struggle can the gospel be heard as the gospel for all.

C. *The Oppressed/Oppressor Dialectic as a Constructive Theological Norm*

It would be indefensible to suggest that, had he lived, Martin Luther King, Jr., would have developed his basic point along the lines that now seem so clear to us. It would also be wide of the mark to suggest that he would not have done so, though it must be noted that at the moment when the civil rights movement deepened into the full-scale Black Revolution an informal division of labor, long overdue, began to assert itself. No longer could multicomponent, charismatic geniuses (and here one thinks not only of King, but also of the towering figure, Malcolm X) carry the burden alone. The labor of serious and prolonged reflective thought—now in order in a new way—could not be developed on the run, between battles and skirmishes, as such books as we have from King were necessarily written. Serious, prolonged, reflective thought can also be aggressive, however, and it has its own decisive role to play in storming the gates of racial oppression. There is no tame, innocuous way to place the oppressed/oppressor dialectic at the head of the agenda of critical, constructive reflection. Vincent Harding's essays form a perfect case in point. So does the emerging theological argument of James Cone, now a professor of theology at Union Theological Seminary in New York.

At this writing Cone has produced three vigorous books that have clearly established him as a force to be reckoned with in American theology. The developing line of argument of these three books turns on the issue now before us. *Black Theology and Black Power* (1969) was Cone's theological manifesto. Early in the initial chapter he insists that "the oppressor is in no position whatever to define the proper response to enslavement," and he focuses this point by asserting: "The real menace in white intellectual arrogance is the dangerous assumption that the structure that enslaves is the structure that will also decide when and how this slavery is to be abolished." [38] Precisely this assumption is the central target of the Black Revolution. "Black Power," as he defines it at the outset of the book, "means black people taking the dominant role in determining the black-white relationship in American society." [39] These fundamental assertions inform Cone's delineation of his basic theological thesis, and his work to date has been devoted to its elaboration:

> It is not my thesis that all Black Power advocates are Christians or even wish to be so. . . . My concern is, rather, to show that the goal and message of Black Power . . . is consistent with the gospel of Jesus Christ. Indeed, I have even suggested that if Christ is present among the oppressed, as he promised, he must be working through the activity of Black Power. This alone is my thesis.[40]

In the initial manifesto Cone's aggressive logic is already intimated. The gospel is correlated with Black Power because Black Power has become the means of coercion by which the case of the oppressed against the oppressor remains in the open. This is its relentless task. The structure that enslaves can take its time with the decision as to *when* and *how* slavery is at last to be eliminated totally. This does not simply aggravate the brutality of the situation. It does far more. It delays interminably any full realization of a glad being in encounter. It does so by adopting a posture of neutrality as regards the social mechanism that perpetuated oppression. As we have seen, Barth's suggestion was that the opposite of "gladly" is "neutrally," and we have argued that a gospel that is neutral on the distortion of the basic form of humanity is no gospel at all. The point simply could not be more germane than it becomes in the situation America has now reached. The use of Black Power as the basic theme of the Black Revolution forces that revolution to its decisive yield, the insistence that says: The gospel cannot be addressed to the need of the oppressed unless it is addressed *in partisan terms.* And this insistence itself carries an immediate corollary: Once the gospel is so addressed, it must be stated in these terms forever.

The relentless unmasking of the fallacy of neutrality is the key to Cone's polemical style, and it is polemics, not rhetoric, that animates his discussions. If the proclamation of the gospel is in the control of oppressors, then this proclamation becomes the tool of oppression. King may have been on his way to seeing and saying this. Cone is saying it now with sharp intensity, and with a broader theological apparatus than King possessed. The target of his theological moves is not the heart and conscience of a white America that should be willing to attempt change peacefully. It is rather the posture of a neutralist theological establishment that must be forced from its dominating position by whatever means necessary. Theological logic, not charismatic persuasion, is the weaponry of this struggle.

In this light, the prevailing characteristic of the content of Cone's theology is both apparent and necessary. It may be typified with a single word, *concreteness.*[41] The partisan proclamation of the gospel is always specific. Indeed, as we have said before, the case can be made that the decisive turnings of the history of Christian thought at large have always been moments of new insistence on the specific concreteness of the gospel that have emerged when theological creativity has been informed by the impasses reached in its living context. To those not disturbed by these impasses, such partisan statements of the gospel will be dismissed as reductions of the universal claims of Christian conviction. To those who are trapped within the devastation of the unbending situation, such partisan statements become the only possible basis on which to mount these universal claims. In America it is the demand of the ethnically oppressed for liberation from this oppression that provides the new occasion for incarnating the grand vision of Christian faith. If the unmasking of the fallacy of neutrality is the key to Cone's polemical style, the singular discipline with which he develops the theme of the concreteness of the gospel is the clue to its content. His second book, *A Black Theology of Liberation* (J. B. Lippincott Company, 1970), takes up in order the long-standing, traditional loci of Christian theology. Far from being a reversion to traditional concerns, however, the discussions of revelation, God, man, Christ, church, world, and eschatology are animated throughout by an initial assertion that is both reminiscent of Barth's insistence on the primacy of Christology for theology as a whole and at the same time directly in touch with the passionate cry for liberation that has always been on the lips of the oppressed.

> Christian theology is a theology of liberation. It is *a rational study of the being of God in the world in light of the existential situation of an oppressed community, relating the forces of liberation to the essence of the gospel, which is Jesus Christ.*[42]

To point to the content of theology in such specific terms carries with it *a double-edged boundary condition.* Both elements are explicitly present in Cone's thought, but for the rather obvious reasons of the polemical situation of the present they are not equally weighted in his current discussions. The dominant element is the exclusion of those who contend against the normative use of the oppressed/

oppressor dialectic. Cone is not willing to relinquish the ground held by the assertion of the black experience as the decisive clue to the gospel in our time and place. He is willing, though, to expand this into the idea of "blackness [as] an ontological symbol," descriptive of "what oppression means in America" and embracing "all people who participate in the liberation of man from oppression." [43] The genius of putting the matter this way is that it deliberately shuns misleading abstraction. Liberation from oppression maintains its definitive role, and all diversions from this overarching concern are unmasked as regressions to the realm of theology as the tool of oppression. In the labors of the theology of the oppressed there is neither time nor room for the distracting attempt to find new topics for a theological agenda dying from the slow fatigue of boredom. This is the import of the invective with which Cone dismissed the "God is dead" theology and the various attempts at a theology of secularization.[44]

Closely related to this, and still part of the dominant element of the double-edged boundary condition of Cone's partisan theology, is the sharp restriction imposed on all tendencies to make "oppression" itself so broad a symbol that the concrete origins of the term can be avoided. Here again we encounter, though now in a much more demanding form, the note so crucial for King, the role of the oppressed in the liberation of the oppressor. Involvement in the actual struggle for liberation is the sole validation of the use of the term "oppression" as a general metaphor comprehending all human needs. This nails to the wall, once and for all, the typical white response to the normative use of the oppressed/oppressor dialectic. "All humanity is oppressed" is the characteristic defensive maneuver. Apart from participation in the struggle for liberation, this assertion leaves things precisely as they are. "The basic difference between black oppression and so-called white oppression," Cone argues, "is the fact that the latter is voluntarily chosen and the former is forced upon the black community." What is at stake here is the inability of oppressors "to know and analyze their slavery." [45] This points to the real battlefront between a theology such as Cone is attempting and the regnant posture of the theological establishment:

> If white intellectuals, religionists, and assorted liberals can convince themselves that the white condition is analogous to the black condition, then there is no reason to respond to the demands of the black community.[46]

As over against this posture (and it embodies the innermost citadel of those whose racism takes the deepest available form—that of regarding ethnic oppression as one of a series of problems), Cone's version of King's gospel unfolds:

> When the oppressed affirm their freedom by refusing to behave according to the masters' rules, they not only liberate themselves from oppression, but they also liberate the oppressors from an enslavement to their illusions.[47]

Only those committed to the actual, visible struggle against concrete oppression can use the term "oppression" as a comprehensive metaphor. For like all metaphors, this too must be derived from the concrete meaning of the term. To speak of the liberation of the Christ apart from such concreteness is to speak of an illusion at the heart of the faith. This is why Cone speaks of the Black Christ, but for the full import of his conviction to be clear we must examine the second element of the twofold limit his partisan theology entails.

It is a colossal mistake to assume, as no doubt most do, that the only offense in speaking of the Black Christ relates to the white community. Here everything depends on perceiving the *full* import of Cone's point regarding "blackness as an ontological symbol" descriptive of all involved in the struggle against oppression. Not all so involved are, or wish to be, Christian—and to those who are not Christian, Cone has a gospel to proclaim. This is a clear implication of the manner in which he begins his first book, and it becomes unmistakably explicit as his writing unfolds:

> Whatever [Black Theology] says about liberation must be said in the light of the black community's experience of Jesus Christ. The failure of many black radicals to win the enthusiasm of the black community may be due to their inability to take seriously the religious character inherent in that community.[48]

This is the point at which Cone's appreciation of King becomes explicit. In his view, what accounts for King's impact on the American scene is the fact that he clearly assumed the intrinsically religious character of the black community and thus insisted that "the 'soul' of the black community is inseparable from liberation but always liberation grounded in Jesus Christ." [49] However, Cone's aggressive attempt to extend the salient won by King not only has him wondering about a gospel of nonviolence in a time that has necessitated the Black Power movement, it also has him distinguishing between the white Jesus and the Black Christ.[50] This distinction, utterly beyond the horizon of King's theology, turns on the insistence that any valid attempt to understand the centrality of Jesus for all Christian thought must entail an explicit relating of "the name [Jesus] to the concrete affairs of men." [51] In our time and place the proclamation of the Christ is the proclamation of a white Christ when it does not relate directly to the struggle for liberation from oppression. To speak of the

Christ in terms of this liberation is to speak of the Black Christ, and this yields what for Cone is "the hermeneutical principle for Black Theology," that is, its guiding principle of interpretation for the understanding of Christianity. The decisive, comprehensive formulation is as follows:

> The norm of Black Theology must take seriously two realities, actually two aspects of a single reality: the liberation of black people and the revelation of Jesus Christ. With these two realities before us, what then is the norm of Black Theology? *The norm of all God-talk which seeks to be black-talk is the manifestation of Jesus as the Black Christ who provides the necessary soul for black liberation.*[52]

A theology so construed informs a gospel to be proclaimed to white and black alike—to whites resisting change, and to blacks whose contention is that the liberation sought can be wrought by human effort alone. Cone, like King, is thus a preacher. The confrontation at the boundary of his theology is double-edged.

The question that now asserts itself must be handled with great care, for it touches on the dynamics of a process now only in its beginning phases, and all that is presently discernible is the commencement of new tasks. The question is simple: Is it possible to go farther than polemics? To refine the question is to encounter its complexity. In refining it, though, it must be obvious that what is *not* being said is that the tension between oppressed and oppressor may be relaxed or ignored. We are not likely to see the time when it may be. Granted this, the refinement is in order, for without it we cannot reckon with the fact that neither Cone nor others of similar mind and soul are willing to accept the salient won in the heat of battle as their final domicile. To refine the question, then, is to ask: Is there a depth to which the partisan theology of the oppressed points that will continue to assert itself when oppression is eradicated? If so, what is it?

Likely to be characteristic of all efforts along this line of inquiry is a genuine ambivalence of expression, necessitated by the fact that the power of the oppressor remains so overwhelming. This power is no less observable within the precincts of the theological establishment than it is elsewhere in the world of white dominance. Accordingly, constructive theological effort utilizing hitherto ignored or suppressed sources of creativity will continue to be combined with the maintenance of polemical pressure, lest the theology of the oppressed be assimilated and thus contained by those who resist the change the oppressed demand. For the polemical struggle the weapons of the opponent are always the most useful. This is probably not the only reason, but surely it is one of the more obvious ones, that lies behind a fact on which we must comment lest our listening to Cone be dismissed as romantically naïve. The theological giants that inform his polemical attack are precisely those that inhabit prominent places in the pantheon of North Atlantic Theology. Withdraw the usual list of Barth, Tillich, Bultmann, Bonhoeffer, and Reinhold Niebuhr from his first two books, and all that remains is the invective of outrage—significant, to be sure, but hardly likely to leave a lasting mark on the theological citadel of oppression. If this is all there is to the partisan theology of the oppressed, then only one prediction is in order: It is doomed to containment. This is not all there is, however, and the question now before us opens the way toward seeing what happens when the theology of the oppressed begins the long offensive beyond the front lines of the initial salient.

The Spirituals and the Blues (1972) marks Cone's initial move beyond the essentially derivative enterprise of polemical combat. To be sure, the aggressive and challenging note remains explicit. How could it be otherwise in any treatment of the origins of the *spirituals* and the *blues* in the suffering of the enslaved and oppressed community? Early in the book Cone rightly insists that the only route into the heart of these lasting expressions of the black experience is that of perceiving the double meaning to be found in virtually every line of these collective yearnings,[53] and the book as a whole is devoted to the exposition of this fact. Now clearly, the appeal to the normative significance of the black experience for theology does not first assert itself in this book, but has rather been present, as we have seen, from Cone's initial manifesto forward. The new emphasis of Cone's third book, however, is the move toward a positive contribution both alongside of and generated by the necessarily polemical stride toward freedom.

A succinct indication of this occurs late in the book, though the intentionality we are noting permeates the argument as a whole. In discussing the meaning of "heaven" in the spirituals, Cone takes up the well-known fact that postponement of deliverance into the great beyond provides a ready means for oppressors to maintain their dominance here and now. Far from being a reason for rejecting the black religion of the heritage of suffering, this provides him with the occasion of refining his understanding of the task of black theologians.

> The task . . . of black theologians is to move beyond the distortions of black religion to the authentic substance of black religious experience so that it can continue to serve as a positive force in liberating black people.[54]

Both at this point and in the subsequent discussion Cone intensifies the note of concreteness on which we have already found him to be so insistent. This leads him to a far-reaching claim. He argues that "The most crucial ingredient of black eschatology was its historicity," and this informs a critical generalization:

> Recently there has been much discussion among American and European theologians about humanizing the world according to God's promised future. But the future about which they speak is too abstract and too unrelated to the history and culture of black people who have been and are being dehumanized and dehistoricized by white imperialists and colonialists. As a black theologian, I believe that authentic Christian hope must be defined by the oppressed's vision of the expectant future and not by philosophical abstractions.[55]

The point at hand both can and must be extrapolated. That it *can* be extrapolated demonstrates that whereas Cone's generalization is critical, it is not restricted to the merely polemical level. That it *must* be extrapolated points to an even more striking fact. Theology thrives on the powers of abstraction, for if it did not, neither the transcending of the mundane nor the pointing toward the ultimate would be possible. The issue is not *whether* abstractions, but *what kind.* The only abstractions available to the theologians of the oppressed are those that are grounded in the reality of the presence of external confines from which the oppressed seek concrete deliverance. The earthiness of theology is thus continually in close juxtaposition with its ethereal propensities. The theology of the oppressed speaks of both the distortion and ruin of humanity and of the awakening and fulfillment of humanity in terms of known realities. The experience of the oppressed forces this by evoking the utilization of the cultural heritage of the oppressed themselves in the process of theological conceptualization.

What now of the question: Is there a depth to which the theology of the oppressed points that will continue to assert itself when oppression is eradicated? If there is not, either oppression will not have been eradicated or it will have returned. That this is not as obvious as it ought to be bears witness to the systemic pervasiveness of the assumption that the Western cultural tradition is not only intrinsically superior to all others, but also capable in and of itself of discerning and resolving all the tensions that undermine human fulfillment. Far more than the work so far accomplished by James Cone is necessary before the full import of the answer to our question can be seen, though it is by no means insignificant that his labors now force and support such a claim.[56]

There is a depth that will continue to assert itself even if oppression does truly disappear. It lies in a new disclosure of reality—the reality of the experience and the promise of the liberated. When this is brought into play with the kind of cogency we have been observing in the work of Cone, the theological enterprise has before it a rich, new option, which it cannot ignore but which it can take up only by moving beyond the frontiers of present theological knowledge. For theological knowledge has not recently been extended by wrestling with its convictions in the midst of the confluence of cultures. It is an open question as to whether it has ever done so where each of the cultures in question knows that common dignity and respect that oppressors fear and therefore deny. The struggle for liberation from ethnic oppression has forced the oppressed/oppressor dialectic into the open at the level of primary consideration. It cannot be treated as if the object were simply to gain new insights for incorporation into a theological apparatus assumed to be basically sound already. The transformation of the entire style of theological reflection is involved.

D. *The Promise*

The promise of mutual interdependence should be obvious by now. It is liberation, and we have been pursuing it throughout this discussion, in following a trail that begins with Barth and moves through King to Cone. This is, of course, only one of the many routes that could have been followed. There are other ways to go, other figures to hear, other discussions that point in the same direction when read in a similar progression. These, however, will suffice, perhaps quite uniquely so, to suggest what is the concrete meaning and portent of saying that liberation is the promise of mutual interdependence. There are at least three vectors, three directed forces, that are discernible in our present discussion, and by lifting them up in turn we shall see why it is that we must move beyond the fixed frontiers of theology as we have known it.

1. *Mutual interdependence promises concrete liberation from oppression because it points the way beyond the oppressed/oppressor contradiction.* Note well: At the moment we can say only that it *points the way.* We are not speaking of an accomplished fact, but of very fragile beginnings, and only if this is clearly acknowledged will the point at hand be kept from deteriorating into an innocuous, repulsive platitude. Theologically speaking, it would be utterly fallacious to suggest that if oppressors realized they have something to gain from liberation, oppression would *ipso facto* disappear. Oppression does not ever automatically disappear. King's warnings and Cone's polemics demonstrate that once and for all. To tame them in the

name of a fallacious hope is to fail to recognize that we are looking toward a promised land we have not yet entered. The point is that we are standing with them in so scanning the horizon, and we can discern the beckoning signals only with the clues they give us.

To grasp the oppressed/oppressor dialectic from within the struggle for liberation is to begin to understand the present reality of the distortion and ruin of the basic form of humanity. For this understanding, those whose heritage is that of the oppressors are categorically dependent upon those whose heritage is the pain of oppression. More than that (though only in the light of that): to become involved in the struggle for liberation is to know the present possibility of the awakening and fulfillment of humanity—an awakening and fulfillment that await *all* who join the struggle, whatever their origins. The new humanity of a different tomorrow than the one that now seems inevitable must be comprised of both the formerly oppressed and the former oppressors. To the insights of the oppressed, then, must be added whatever the sons and daughters of oppressors can bring with them from the arsenal of oppression for the widening front of the battle for deliverance. It is risky to put the matter this bluntly, for inevitably such a statement will incur wrath from all quarters. The risk must be run, however, precisely because of the thrust of the arguments of Martin King and James Cone. To place the oppressed/oppressor dialectic at the head of the theological agenda is to insist that even giants such as Troeltsch and Barth can be, and are being, bent to the service of oppression. At the same time it is to insist that their prior labors can be appropriated now in the effort to carry the theology of the oppressed beyond the frontiers of the present struggle. Mindful of the fragile character of all new beginnings, and thus with fear and trembling, we must take up the task of mutual *inter*-dependence. A new tomorrow is at hand. Mutual interdependence points the way toward it.

2. *Mutual interdependence unmasks the negative possibility of mutual intelligibility.* Mutual intelligibility, even as we have attempted to construe it, can serve oppression. It is possible to listen to the other in order more efficiently to reduce him or her to an object. I-Thou language on the lips of an oppressor is an obscenity because it masks the attempt to contain the revolutionary portent of every effort to treat all men and women as Thou's. The wise among the oppressors are those who listen, carefully and with the pose of compassion, to the very figures we have heard, precisely in order to keep them in the place of inferiority. Mutual intelligibility, we can now say, thus has a double capacity. Mutual interdependence is accordingly a critical principle, not a pious hope. It forces a decision for the positive—and against the negative—possibility of the use of mutual intelligibility.

Mutual intelligibility turns on the perception of difference. The trouble is that the perception of difference has always generated compulsive value judgments, the passion to be satisfied as to which is the superior of two or more differing individualities (in Troeltsch's sense of the term).[57] Mutual interdependence as a critical principle has to do with the *relocation* of the question of value. It relocates this question forever by placing it in the unfolding reality of *reciprocal exchange.* If the plane of mutual intelligibility has been reached, the way is open to exclude all denials of pluralism. But since *the* issue that emerges on this plane is incarnated in the oppressed/oppression dialectic, all denials of the concrete struggle for liberation are also rejected. Now it is decisive to understand that the brutal range of the distortion and ruin of the basic form of humanity is most evident at this second remove. Given mutual intelligibility,

to deny pluralism is blindness. Given mutual interdependence, to utilize pluralism for the perpetuation of oppression
is the threshold of sin—not the simple error of those who do
nothing because they do not know, but the profound
distortion of those who do nothing even though they do
know, and thus settle for the demonic identity of the I-It
world.

3. *Mutual interdependence describes the liberation of life
and thought in the plural world.* To move beyond the
oppressed/oppressor contradiction is not to move into a
homogenous realm. To construe the new reality as homogenous would be to reduplicate oppression. To move beyond
the oppressed/oppressor contradiction is to move into the
realm of multiple realities which are dependent upon each
other for the intertwining, unfolding realizations of liberated identities—into, that is, the world of the awakening
and fulfillment of humanity.

It may be that the specific task of life and thought in the
American context is to understand and proclaim this, for the
possibility of the celebration of the plurality of humanity in
all its forms is uniquely present where the *ethnic* plurality of
humanity is visible and unavoidable. Here the theological
enterprise is confronted by a necessity that can become a
privilege—that of a radical, new move through the opening
of untried cultural exchanges. If this occurs, a contribution
to the broader, global plurality that is humanity as a whole
in its yearning for ultimacy will have unfolded. For if this
occurs, theology will have placed its rich treasure at the
disposal of an emerging new order, not as a master seeking
to control, but as a co-laborer seeking to discover a shared
redemption. How radically in our time and place must
we—can we—peer into the depths of the ancient saying,
"Behold, the kingdom of God is in the midst of you" (Luke
17:21)?

4:
SENSITIVITY TO VARYING RATES OF RELATABILITY

THE DISCIPLINE OF MUTUAL INTELLIGIBILITY AND THE promise of mutual interdependence describe the route along which the theological enterprise will move if it hears the haunting insistence of Du Bois with which we began our reflections. Far more should now be apparent as the import of saying that "the problem of the Twentieth Century is the problem of the color line." This is not simply the agonized cry of a brilliant spokesman of and for the downtrodden. It is the formulation of the opportunity for the expansion of human liberation beyond humanity's grandest dreams. To take the problem of the color line seriously—that is, to regard it as the problem that informs all other problems—is to move into the world of manifold, oscillating relationships that we have used the phrase "ethnic pluralism" to describe. The world of manifold patterns of relationships is one in which intelligibility serves interdependence, not dominance; i.e., one listens in order not to conquer but to relate.

When mutual intelligibility serves mutual interdependence, the possibility of reciprocating creativity becomes real. The realm of reciprocal creativity, however, is not simple but complex, and our efforts toward such creativity will be to no avail if we do not discern this with precision.

In order to discern this, we must observe the fact that within the realm of theological pluralism there are at least two crucial parameters, without an awareness of which the dream of reciprocal creativity will remain only an elusive fantasy. These are indicated by the phrases "varying rates of relatability" and "mutual openness to change." The first has to do with the spectrum of sensitivity that theological pluralism must maintain. The second has to do with the integrity of purpose that theological pluralism must envision. We may state the point at which we have arrived in the following formula: Mutual Intelligibility plus Mutual Interdependence yields Reciprocal Creativity. But we must now deal with the fact that if this formula is to be descriptive of an *inexhaustible* continuum, the operation of these two parameters must be described and promoted. We shall treat the first of these parameters in this chapter, basing the point on the red side of the red/white/black triangle. We shall treat the second parameter in the final chapter, where, once again, we shall have the triangle as a whole before us.

A. *The Red Religion of the Land*

The dignity of American Indians is not a new fact; it is hoary with age. As we have seen, what is new in these most recent years is that it is being asserted in the open and with newfound vigor by *Indian* speakers. That which has always been known in the tribes is now becoming available, on an increasingly broadening scale, to all who have ears to hear. This is not to say that white scholarship has ignored the Native American—the bibliographies are immense. Nor is it to say that the white scholarly attempt has been utterly devoid of profoundly sympathetic efforts. John Neihardt's disciplined and sensitive *Black Elk Speaks* (originally published in 1932) and Frank Waters' *Book of the Hopi* (originally published in 1963) are splendid cases in point. Neihardt's work places before us the life and thought of a holy man of the Oglala Sioux, and Waters' efforts leave recorded in writing the total religious outlook of the Hopi people as this has been gleaned, carefully, painstakingly, and in great detail, from "some thirty elders of the Hopi Indian tribe in Northern Arizona." [1] As we shall see, to know these works is to know that the debt to Neihardt and Waters is incalculable. And surely a similar remark is in order regarding Dee Brown's widely read *Bury My Heart at Wounded Knee* (Holt, Rinehart & Winston, Inc., 1970), which for the first time has set the record straight, with dreadful precision, regarding the white invasion of the American plains. Properly studied, these three works could trigger a profound transformation in the way in which white—and black—Americans understand the red brothers and sisters whose heritage in America antedates theirs by millennia.

The astonishing thing is that works such as these three can now be *properly* studied by non-Indian readers—for the first time in years, perhaps for the first time ever. For out of the struggles that have yielded the ethnic revolutions defining today's America have arisen Indian voices that are willing to take the risk of speaking beyond the boundaries of tribal identity to all who can be commanded to listen. To *hear* them is to approach works such as we have cited with an eye toward tomorrow, not yesterday, precisely in accord with the intentionality of these three perceptive white authors. Apart from the urgent pressure of Indian assertions of *contemporary* red dignity, even treatises that have the integrity of the three books just mentioned are likely to be misused. They are likely to be consigned to an avocational fascination with the discovery of a true past, rather than appropriated for the revolutionary effort to build a new future. In its own way this observation epitomizes all that we have attempted to clarify regarding intelligibility and interdependence, but the depth and the complexity of what is involved will be perceived only if we are willing to listen long to what the red brothers and sisters have to say. For they speak *from within* (not *about*) the dignity inherent in an ancient birthright. The stories they have to tell are manifold and complicated. They must be heard in some detail, or not at all.

The religion of the red brothers and sisters is the religion of the land. It is absolutely necessary that we grasp the full import of this fact. But lest we succumb to the misleading fascination with the past we must make clear at the outset a controlling assumption. It is this: In that *all* American Indians are tribal men and women, the heritage of the religion of the land is, in one way or another, *formatively significant* for each of them. No white imperialism, within or without the churches, has ever succeeded in diminishing the intensity of this central component of the red birthright. The lands of the Indian were taken, but tribal identity survived. Accordingly, the transition of Indians into the churches served only to generate a deep trauma that has now come into the open with new forcefulness. It meant that red men and women became bi-religious, but they were never permitted to unfold the unique insights this could yield. Thus the decisive issue emerges. Precisely because the issue is tomorrow, not yesterday, the overcoming of the longstanding frustration of Indian creativity is the sole point to wrestling with the depths of the fact that the religion of the Indians is the religion of the land. This creativity, like all creativity, must be free—free to go wheresoever it will. For some it will mean an explicit rejection of the religion of the white invaders in favor of an equally explicit return to the religions of the tribes. For others it will mean the taking up of a long-denied task—the forging of a genuinely tribal version of the gospel of Jesus the Christ. But for each what we must now see is all-pervasive. No effort to understand either of these options as they simultaneously take shape can be successful without a grasp of the range and the portent of the heritage of the religion of the land.

Three factors make the task here envisioned a difficult one: (1) the enduring Christian assumption that the legends, stories, and ceremonies embodying the religions of the tribes may be immediately dismissed because they are obviously pagan; (2) the fact of the multiplicity of the tribes themselves; and (3) the virtual impossibility of recovering the original religions in any final detail, since they lived and live in oral traditions that have now been buffeted for centuries. Each of these factors will haunt our constructive efforts unless they are dealt with explicitly as we begin our attempt to understand.

The first of these factors is probably self-evident, given all that we have seen so far. It demands attention, however, since it is the domicile of a lasting resentment that inhibits the theological creativity so urgently needed now. Though there well may have been noble exceptions to the general rule, the early Christian missionaries seem to have made no effort to *hear* the enthusiasm of red men and women for their own religious traditions. Writing in 1911, a remarkable Sioux, Charles Alexander Eastman, recalled a scene that apparently strikes a responsive chord in the recollections of all the tribes:

A missionary once undertook to instruct a group of Indians in the truths of his holy religion. He told them of the creation of the earth in six days, and of the fall of our first parents by eating an apple.

The courteous savages listened attentively, and, after thanking him, one related in his turn a very ancient tradition concerning the origin of the maize. But the missionary plainly showed his disgust and disbelief, indignantly saying:

"What I delivered to you were scared truths, but this that you tell me is mere fable and falsehood!"

"My brother," gravely replied the offended Indian, "it seems that you have not been well grounded in the rules of civility. You saw that we, who practice these rules, believed your stories; why, then, do you refuse to credit ours?" [2]

Why indeed! Little is to be gained in lamenting now the intransigent rigidity of that spokesman for the gospel. For if that is the only response to the recounting of this and countless other similar scenes the issue will be left in the past, and the present will remain under the myopic control of what we have earlier called North Atlantic Theology. What is at stake is our own complete renunciation of the position taken by that missionary. The deep irony is that Christianity, itself the ongoing unfolding of myriad combinations of the gospel and cultural forms, simply and categorically refused to entertain the possibility of a new permutation in exchanges with the religions of the tribes. The bitter reality now is that it cannot do so in the present, nor can it encourage today's red brothers and sisters to work along the lines of such a dialogue, without the genuine willingness to struggle to discern where true affinities lie and actually new possibilities are to be found. Earlier in our discussion we heard Deloria speak of such a possibility and why it has never come to pass. [3]

The second complicating factor involved in any contemporary attempt to hear the theological contribution of the red brothers and sisters has to do with the multiplicity of the tribes. We have already heard Vine Deloria, Jr., protest the stereotypes that reduce all Indians to a monolithic entity.

Important though this is, however, it can be misleading in unexpected ways when one takes up the task of coming to an understanding of the red religion of the land. The immediate inclination is to think that whereas there is an emerging *black theology* one can rightly speak only of *red theologies*. In this vein, so the argument would run, to speak of red theology would be to mount a series of generalizations that will not be countenanced within the plural ferment of the tribes themselves. Now certainly, there is much to say for this line of argument. The beginning of wisdom in the matter of hearing the theology of the red brothers and sisters is the recognition of the fact that every American Indian does his or her thinking as a member of a given tribe, and that this will decisively condition any given individual participation in genuinely Indian theological creativity now. This is, however, only the *beginning* of wisdom. If the issue were only one of recovering the past it could be left here. The issue is not the past alone, however. Any overemphasis on the fact of the multiplicity of the tribes threatens to confine Indian theological reflection to the passion for repristination. And if this passion rules, the theology of oppressors simply remains intact. The purpose of hearing today's red thinkers is not a repaired yesterday, but a new tomorrow—one in which the fallacy of the theology of oppressors has been exposed by new currents of thought.

Deloria has moved to a sharpened articulation of this point in his fourth and most recent book, *God Is Red* (1973). That an aroused interest in American Indians is now widespread is clear, judging by the expanding market for anthologies of excerpts of speeches and stories from the past experience of the tribes. But, as Deloria notes, "The tragedy of America's Indians—that is, the Indians that America loves and loves to read about—is that they no longer exist, except in the pages of books." [4] And this uncovers the issue. Immense effort on the part of red men and women will always be needed in resisting their confinement to the stereotyped image of "the American Indian." Precisely this effort informs much of Deloria's writing in his first two books. What we have called the new emergence of red dignity specifically involves recognition of the spectrum of the tribes. In *God Is Red*, however, Deloria has moved on to deal with the ironic result which this recognition has yielded.

> For most of the century it has been necessary for people of the different tribes to keep reminding non-Indians that all tribes are different, that they have different histories, different languages, different cultural values, and different religions. So thoroughly entrenched has this idea become, even among Indians, that it has been virtually a gospel that no sense can be made of the general topic of Indians, but each and every peculiarity and distinction must be emphasized to interpret correctly tribal uniqueness.[5]

Hence the problem. In the face of this, Indians and non-Indians alike can fail to recognize what it is that the tribes have had in common for nearly four hundred years—i.e., their resistance to the white invader.

> The one common thing that each tribe experienced was its invasion of its homeland by western European white men. The similarity in the speeches is not accidental, therefore, in an important aspect. Almost every speech was given on the occasion in which the tribe was confronted with the need to respond to a consistent opposing force that immediately threatened tribal existence. While we can affirm that all tribes have uniqueness with respect to their attitudes toward the federal government, missionaries, and white society in general, the same basic response was made. It is possible, in this sense, to identify an "Indianness" which is intimately

shared by all American Indian people—the response made to white society.[6]

One must know the tribes in order to discern the development of the trans-tribal view Deloria here envisions. But only by way of this new development will the multiplicity of the tribes yield that new contribution intrinsic to a theology in red, white, and black. Without it, today's Indian creativity will be restricted to the insights of a museum guide.

To the two complicating factors before us we must add a rather obvious third: there is no way back to the original religions of the tribes. We are faced, rather, with the necessity of dealing with recollections that have filtered through the experience of the tribes in their efforts to survive the white invaders. This was carefully indicated decades ago in the writing of Charles Alexander Eastman (1858–1939). Born a Santee Dakota (his Sioux name was Ohiyesa) and raised in his tribe, this remarkable figure graduated from Dartmouth in 1887, and three years later received his M.D. from Boston University. His *The Soul of the Indian* (1911), which we have already cited, is invaluable for our present efforts. In approaching the subject of "Ceremonial and Symbolic Worship" he delineates the problem as follows:

> The public religious rites of the Plains Indians are few, and in large part of modern origin belonging properly to the so-called "transition period." That period must be held to begin with the first insidious effect upon their manners and customs of contact with the dominant race, and many of the tribes were so influenced long before they ceased to lead the nomadic life.
>
> The fur-traders, the "Black Robe" priests, the military, and finally the Protestant missionaries, were the men who began the disintegration of the Indian nations and the

overthrow of their religion, seventy-five to a hundred years before they were forced to enter upon reservation life. We have no authentic study of them until well along in the transition period, when whiskey and trade had already debauched their native ideals.[7]

The significance of this third factor is at least twofold. Characteristically, white concern over the tragic impasse of American Indians can take an exclusively historical shape. New efforts at constructive theological exchange with tribal ideas must expect, therefore, the charge that the original religions of the tribes were not what the proponents of such efforts say they were. To this, then, must be added the continuum of futility that those who would speak for the depth of tribal religions seem always to have known when attempting to set out what the old ones taught them. This note is surely present in the closing lines of *The Soul of the Indian:*

> Such are the beliefs in which I was reared—the secret ideals which have nourished in the American Indian a unique character among the peoples of the earth. Its simplicity, its reverence, its bravery and uprightness must be left to make their own appeal to the American of to-day, who is the inheritor of our homes, our names, and our traditions. Since there is nothing left us but remembrance, at least let that remembrance be just! [8]

Much more, however, than the case for just remembrance is at hand in works such as Eastman's. Ours is a time when this can lead to the labor attending new developments, in the face of which neither white complacency nor red hopelessness may be permitted to obstruct the coming of a new day.

With all this before us, we turn now to ponder the religion of the land. The tribal religions were and remain religions of the land because they were and remain religions of nature. Of this there can be no doubt. It is one of the clearest and most basic motifs to filter through what Eastman called the time of transition. The literature here is vast, and within the scope of our present undertaking we can do no more than sample it. We shall do so by examining first the point of departure of Eastman's *The Soul of the Indian*. In this light we shall then turn to Neihardt's *Black Elk Speaks*. These are key sources for the Sioux background against which Deloria's effort in *God Is Red* may be discerned, and this effort will be one of the sources before us in our concluding chapter. However, in that we must come to terms there with what is now taking shape as a trans-tribal contribution to the theology of the present we must at least suggest affinities between these Sioux perspectives and those of other tribes. To be sure, we must ultimately do much more than is possible here, but to this end we shall find help in Waters' *Book of the Hopi*.

Eastman began *The Soul of the Indian* with a discussion of "The Great Mystery." From other sources one knows his reference to be to *Wakan Tanka*.[9] The name is properly translated "Great Mystery," as by Eastman, or "The Great Mysterious One," as by Neihardt,[10] not "Great Spirit" as the white stereotype would have it, though apparently the context sometimes calls for the latter translation.[11] Eastman notes early in his book, at a point where he states his mystification at the profane and sacrilegious language of white men: "In our own tongue His name was not spoken aloud, even with utmost reverence, much less lightly or irreverently." [12] Eastman would have his reader understand that *the* clue to everything else in the religion of his tribe was the basic attitude toward the Great Mystery. The initial formulation of this controls the book as a whole.

> The worship of the "Great Mystery" was silent, solitary, free from all self-seeking. It was silent, because all speech is of

necessity feeble and imperfect; therefore the souls of my ancestors ascended to God in wordless adoration. It was solitary, because they believed that He is nearer to us in solitude, and there were no priests authorized to come between a man and his Maker. None might exhort or confess or in any way meddle with the religious experience of another. Among us all men were created sons of God and stood erect, as conscious of their divinity. Our faith might not be formulated in creeds, nor forced upon any who were unwilling to receive it; hence there was no preaching, proselyting, nor persecution, neither were there any scoffers or atheists.

There were no temples or shrines among us save those of nature.[13]

Pervading the entirety of the outlook of the tribe, the sense of life before the Great Mystery was decisive for the life of the tribe as a whole. Its most intense experience, however, was in what Eastman calls "solitary communion with the Unseen," [14] and as such it informed the rite of passage into maturity. This is the *vision quest*, which in one way or another figures in the life of all the tribes.[15] Eastman's portrayal of this is both memorable and of critical significance for our own discussion. He unfolds it by way of clarifying for his readers the word *hambeday*, "literally 'mysterious feeling,' which has been variously translated 'fasting' and 'dreaming.' It may better be interpreted as 'consciousness of the divine.' " [16] The portrayal of the vision quest then follows, and we must have it before us in detail.

The first *hambeday*, or religious retreat, marked an epoch in the life of the youth, which may be compared to that of confirmation or conversion in Christian experience. Having first prepared himself by means of the purifying vapor-bath, and cast off as far as possible all human or fleshly influences, the young man sought out the noblest height, the most commanding summit in all the surrounding region. Knowing that God sets no value upon material things, he took with him no offerings or sacrifices other than symbolic objects, such as paints and tobacco. Wishing to appear before Him in all humility, he wore no clothing save his moccasins and breech-clout. At the solemn hour of sunrise or sunset he took up his position, overlooking the glories of earth and facing the "Great Mystery," and there he remained, naked, erect, silent, and motionless, exposed to the elements and forces of His arming, for a night and a day to two days and nights, but rarely longer. Sometimes he would chant a hymn without words, or offer the ceremonial "filled pipe." In this holy trance or ecstasy the Indian mystic found his highest happiness and the motive power of his existence.[17]

Given the year in which this was written, it is not surprising to find Eastman paralleling the vision quest to confirmation or conversion. Later in his discussion he likewise compares the two crucial items of the *vapor-bath* and the *filled pipe*, both central for the religious practices of the Sioux and involved in the portrayal before us, to baptism and holy communion.[18] This probably does not bear analysis, and when we take account of the effort at contemporary American Indian religious thought, with its complete absence of any penchant for suggesting such parallels, we could be reminded of Vincent Harding's delineation of the transition in our time from Negro to Black History. Be that as it may, the base upon which we must build in order to reckon with American Indian religious thought today is before us in Eastman's portrayal of the Indian mystic, and in this connection there is one point at which his willingness to find parallels with Christianity is decisive. The religion of nature is not the worship of nature. It is rather, to use Eastman's phrase, "solitary communion with the Unseen" by means of nature. "The rites of this physical worship . . . were wholly symbolic, and the Indian no more worshiped the Sun than the Christian adores the Cross." [19]

Black Elk was Eastman's contemporary, though there is no apparent indication that they knew each other. There is no reason that they should have. The Sioux tribe, which is how white men knew it, is itself a composite of many parts. The Sioux called themselves *Lakota* (or *Nakota*, or *Dakota*, depending upon the branch of the broader tribe in question), and the meaning of their word is "the allies." [20] Black Elk tells us, "I am a Lakota of the Oglala band." [21] Eastman, as we have seen, was a Santee Dakota. Black Elk was born in 1863.[22] He was a second cousin of the celebrated Crazy Horse.[23] We know him because of the remarkable book by John G. Neihardt, entitled, *Black Elk Speaks: Being the Life Story of a Holy Man of the Oglala Sioux, as told through John G. Neihardt (Flaming Rainbow)*.[24] What emerges in this book is a full-bodied example of the Indian mystic as described by Eastman.

Neihardt first met Black Elk in August of 1930. The prolonged conversations yielding the book took place in May of 1931 (the book was first published in 1932).[25] Central for Black Elk's story and for our concerns is the recounting of "The Great Vision," but we must note carefully that this is being interpreted from the vantage point of the closing years of a long life. Black Elk himself calls attention to this. He states that the vision occurred when he was nine years old, during a time when he was sick for twelve days. He recalls when he responded to the treatment of the medicine man:

> As I lay there thinking about the wonderful place where I had been and all that I had seen, I was very sad; for it seemed to me that everybody ought to know about it, but I

was afraid to tell, because I knew that nobody would believe me, little as I was. . . .[26]

Now nearing his seventies, he reflected on this:

I am sure now that I was then too young to understand it all, and that I only felt it. It was the pictures I remembered and the words that went with them; for nothing I have ever seen with my eyes was so clear and bright as what my vision showed me; and no words that I have ever heard with my ears were like the words I heard. I did not have to remember these things; they have remembered themselves all these years. It was as I grew older that the meanings came clearer and clearer out of the pictures and the words; and even now I know that more was shown to me than I can tell.[27]

In the presence of this remark the already insoluble problem of making any comprehensive generalizations about mystical experiences is intensified, for here we are dealing with a continuum of experience, all of which is read back into the structure of an early vision. One thing, though, is clear. The vision supplied the means by which Black Elk understood the life of his tribe, and thus his own life, before the Great Mystery. The vision as a whole is far too complex to be susceptible to a simple recapitulation,[28] and obviously, only those with a deep knowledge of the Sioux experience can offer any lasting commentary on the meaning of its many components. Some of these, however, are of immediately apparent significance for what we are trying to understand.

In its barest essentials, the vision finds Black Elk summoned by two men into the presence of the Six Grandfathers. These "were not old men, but the Powers of the World. And the first was the Power of the West; the second, of the North; the third, of the East; the fourth, of

the South; the fifth, of the Sky; the sixth, of the Earth."
From each of these, in turn, Black Elk received the powers
of life. From the West, the wooden cup of water, and the
bow—the power to make live, and the power to destroy.
From the North, the white giant's wing (the wing of the
white goose)—the power of "the cleansing wind." From
the East, the pipe with the spotted eagle outstretched upon
the stem—the power of peace, and of healing. From the
South, the vision of the nation's hoop, and of the two roads,
and with these, the power to grow.

We must linger for a moment at the gift of the Fourth
Grandfather, for in many ways it is the heart of the vision as
a whole, and certainly it is the clue to all that follows. It
unfolds in two parts, and we need each of them in detail.

> And now the fourth Grandfather spoke, he of the place
> where you are always facing (the south), whence comes the
> power to grow. "Younger brother," he said, "with the
> powers of the four quarters you shall walk, a relative.
> Behold, the living center of a nation I shall give you, and
> with it many you shall save." And I saw that he was holding
> in his hand a bright red stick that was alive, and as I looked it
> sprouted at the top and sent forth branches, and on the
> branches many leaves came out and murmured and in the
> leaves the birds began to sing. And then for just a little while
> I thought I saw beneath it in the shade the circled villages of
> people and every living thing with roots or legs or wings, and
> all were happy. "It shall stand in the center of the nation's
> circle," said the Grandfather, "a cane to walk with and a
> people's heart; and by your powers you shall make it
> bloom." [29]

First, then, there is the holy stick that becomes a tree,
around which the people and all living things are circled.
Also involved, however, is an explication of the experience
of the tribe, caught up in the symbolism of *the two roads*,
and in the introduction of *the four ascents:*

Then when he had been still a little while to hear the birds sing, he spoke again: "Behold the earth!" So I looked down and saw it lying yonder like a hoop of peoples, and in the center bloomed the holy stick that was a tree, and where it stood there crossed two roads, a red one and a black. "From where the giant lives (the north) to where you always face (the south) the red road goes, the road of good," the Grandfather said, "and on it shall your nation walk. The black road goes from where the thunder beings live (the west) to where the sun continually shines (the east), a fearful road, a road of troubles and of war. On this also you shall walk, and from it you shall have the power to destroy a people's foes. In four ascents you shall walk the earth with power."

I think he meant that I should see four generations, counting me, and now I am seeing the third.[30]

The Fifth and Sixth Grandfathers, the Power of the Sky and the Power of the Earth, summon Black Elk to the wanderings that yield insight into the experience of the tribe. The Fifth Grandfather enables him to go across the earth and behold all of it, and in the Sixth Grandfather, Black Elk discerns himself in old age: "I stared at him, for it seemed I knew him somehow; and as I stared, he slowly changed, for he was growing backwards into youth, and when he had become a boy, I knew that he was myself with all the years that would be mine at last." [31] The vision now recounts his wanderings, which are vast, and ultimately, upon his return to the Six Grandfathers, he is greeted with the words: "Grandson, all over the universe you have seen. Now you shall go back with power to the place from whence you came, and it shall happen yonder that hundreds shall be sacred, hundreds shall be flames! Behold!" [32]

Central to the wanderings is the establishment of the nation's hoop, an exact acting out of the gift of the Fourth

Grandfather. Prompted by a voice saying, "Behold, they have given you the center of the nation's hoop to make it live," [33] Black Elk rides to the center of the village and there gives the gathered people the sacred pipe and the wing of the white giant. Then follows the high moment:

> I took the bright red stick and at the center of the nation's hoop I thrust it in the earth. As it touched the earth it leaped mightily in my hand and was a waga chun, the rustling tree [the cottonwood], very tall and full of leafy branches and of all birds singing. And beneath it all the animals were mingling with the people like relatives and making happy cries. The women raised their tremolo of joy, and the men shouted all together: "Here we shall raise our children and be as little chickens under the mother sheo's [the prairie hen's] wing." [34]

Shortly after this comes the interpretation of *the four ascents.* The first culminates in a green land, with the nation's hoop intact. The second finds the tribe still on the red road, but the culmination knows voices of trouble, and now the leaves begin to fall from the holy tree.

As we have heard him say it, Black Elk concluded that he would see four generations, and that as he tells the vision to Neihardt he is seeing the third. Accordingly, it is with the delineation of the third ascent that the turning point of the vision is reached. The people now travel the black road, the road of trouble, and confusion and chaos is at hand.

> And the Voice said: "Behold your nation, and remember what your Six Grandfathers gave you, for thenceforth your people walk in difficulties."
>
> Then the people broke camp again, and saw the black road before them towards where the sun goes down, and black clouds coming yonder; and they did not want to go but could not stay. And as they walked the third ascent, all the animals and fowls that were the people ran here and there, for each one seemed to have his own little vision that he

followed and his own rules; and all over the universe I could hear the winds at war like wild beasts fighting.[35]

Worse than this, the nation's hoop was now broken, and this symbolized the dreadful portent lying ahead, in the fourth generation Black Elk would see:

> And when we reached the summit of the third ascent and camped, the nation's hoop was broken like a ring of smoke that spreads and scatters and the holy tree seemed dying and all its birds were gone. And when I looked ahead I saw that the fourth ascent would be terrible.[36]

Beyond this point in the vision Black Elk speaks his hopes, not his recapitulation of the experience of the tribe as he had known it. The scene is depicted on a grand scale, and it contains a note of universalism that bespeaks a trans-tribal passion emerging from the destruction through which he had seen his tribe pass within the span of his own lifetime. Black Elk is taken to a high mountain to observe "the whole hoop of the world." Commenting on this in a note, Neihardt recalls that "Black Elk said the mountain he stood upon in his vision was Harney Peak in the Black Hills. 'But anywhere is the center of the world,' he added." [37] The remark is significant in that it makes explicit the composite character of "The Great Vision" as Black Elk recounted it to Neihardt in 1931. This is of a piece with the observation with which we began, namely, that the vision itself became the vehicle for Black Elk's total grasp of the life of his tribe, and of his own self-understanding, before the Great Mystery. Moreover, it adds depth to the last scene we shall quote, for it contains a hope worthy of consideration by all who would move beyond the destructive oppression of our time.

> Then a Voice said: "Behold this day, for it is yours to make. Now you shall stand upon the center of the earth to see, for there they are taking you."

I was still on my bay horse, and once more I felt the riders of the west, the north, the east, the south, behind me in formation, as before, and we were going east. I looked ahead and saw the mountains there with rocks and forests on them, and from the mountains flashed all colors upward to the heavens. Then I was standing on the highest mountain of them all, and round about beneath me was the whole hoop of the world. And while I stood there I saw more than I can tell and I understood more than I saw; for I was seeing in a sacred manner the shapes of all things in the spirit, and the shape of all shapes as they must live together like one being. And I saw that the sacred hoop of my people was one of many hoops that made one circle, wide as daylight and as starlight, and in the center grew one mighty flowering tree to shelter all the children of one mother and one father. And I saw that it was holy.[38]

Such, then, in brief scope is Black Elk's vision. We can perceive in it 'the composite yield of what, following Eastman, is the creativity of the Indian mystic. Through the prism of his own imagination Black Elk focused the religious heritage of his tribe, its legends and its ceremonies, and forged these, along with his own understanding of the generations he had seen, into a comprehensive schema of interpretation which is epic in intentionality if not in articulation. The world of nature, as he knew it, and the dependence of his tribe and of himself upon nature, as he celebrated it, were the building blocks of his reflection, and the suffering experienced by his people informed the yearning of his ultimate hopes—hopes that cannot fail to be moving when carefully studied.

The task of working out clear demonstrations of the parallels between the religions of the tribes is far too complicated and tenuous to be undertaken here, and it could well be that the time in fact has not yet arrived for this effort, since many more *Indian* speakers must be heard than have yet spoken if the precision needed for concluding neither too much nor too little is to be gained. However, certain very real affinities can be discerned. When one turns from Eastman and Black Elk to Frank Waters' *Book of the Hopi* these abound.

In the late 1950's, over a three-year period, Waters, with the indispensable assistance of a member of the Hopi tribe, Oswald White Bear Fredericks, set out to record, translate, organize, and publish the recollections of thirty Hopi elders. This effort yielded, in 1963, the *Book of the Hopi.* Waters' organization of the material for publication reflected his contention that, read in proper sequence, "it virtually constitutes a Hopi Bible." [39] This is a bold claim indeed, and one wonders whether Hopi people themselves give it their full assent, for whereas the materials are drawn from Hopi spokesmen and spokeswomen, the arrangement of them is Waters' own. Even so, to follow his presentation step by step is to encounter, in turn, (1) the *four myths* relating the successive creation of the four worlds, in the fourth of which the tribe now lives; (2) the *legends* setting out the migrations of the clans, culminating in their arrival in their present lands; (3) the *mystery plays*, the ceremonies of the clans, which, taken together, are "an annual cycle of nine great religious ceremonies that dramatize the universal laws of life";[40] and (4) the *history,* with its unfulfilled prophecy of "the lost white brother." [41]

The detailed analysis of this sweep of material is clearly beyond the scope of our present undertaking. It would entail an even more complicated recounting than we have followed in setting out something of Black Elk's vision, for here we have access to the recollections of a tribe, not just of an individual. What we can discern, however, is that the key feature on which the myths and the ceremonies turn is the idea of *emergence*, which idea also informs the construction of the *kiva*, the "underground ceremonial chamber," [42] that plays such a decisive role in the life of the tribe.

Central to the four myths is the transition from one world to the next. When evil appears in the first world, the tribe itself is gathered. It consists of what can only be construed as a faithful remnant (and for all that follows it is crucial to know that "the word 'Hopi' means 'peace.' ").[43] The tribe is summoned by the central figure of the myths, Sótuknang.

Among all the people of different races and languages there were a few in every group who still lived by the laws of Creation. To them came Sótuknang. He came with the sound as of a mighty wind and suddenly appeared before them. He said, "I have observed this state of affairs. It is not good. It is so bad I talked to my Uncle, Taiowa, about it. We have decided this world must be destroyed and another one created so you people can start over again. You are the ones we have chosen." [44]

Sótuknang is sent by Taiowa, the Creator. We first hear of him at the outset of the myth of the first world. Sótuknang is the agent of Taiowa's plan for the creation. Here, now, we watch him arrange for the safeguarding of the people while he proceeds to the destruction of the first world. In the passages that follow we obviously have before us one version of the origin of kiva,[45] and an indication of how the myths were used to communicate basic ethical concerns.

He led them to a big mound where the Ant People lived, stamped on the roof, and commanded the Ant People to open up their home. When an opening was made on top of the anthill Sótuknang said to the people, "Now you will enter this Ant kiva, where you will be safe when I destroy the world. While you are here I want you to learn a lesson from these Ant People." [46]

Sótuknang now proceeds to destroy the first world by fire. During their sojourn with the Ant People, the people learn industriousness and forethought, and they recall Sótuknang's words, "[The Ant People] live peacefully with one another. They obey the plan of Creation." [47] Above all the people learn the willingness of the Ant People to share their food.

> "Do not give us so much of the food you have worked so hard to gather and store," the people said.
> "Yes, you are our guests," the Ant people told them. "What we have is yours also." So the Ant People continued to deprive themselves of food in order to supply their guests. Every day they tied their belts tighter and tighter. That is why ants today are so small around the waist.[48]

Then, the destruction being completed, and the second world having been made, the people are summoned:

> When all was ready [Sótuknang] came to the roof of the Ant kiva, stamped on it, and gave his call. Immediately the Chief of the Ant People went up to the opening and rolled back the *nuta* [i.e., the straw thatch over the ladder opening of a Hopi kiva]. "*Yung-ai!* Come in! You are welcome!" he called.[49]

The Ant People are praised and sent forth into the second world as ants, and the people are admonished to "multiply and be happy. But remember your Creator and the laws he gave you. When I hear you singing joyful praises to him I will know you are my children, and you will be close to me in your hearts." [50]

The transition to the third world is analogous to what we have just seen. When trouble, wars between the villages, and wickedness appear, Taiowa and Sótuknang decide on the destruction of the second world, this time by ice. Again the people are sent to dwell with the Ant People, and again the sharing of food is emphasized. And as before, after the destruction had taken place, and then the creation of the third world, the people are summoned and similarly admonished, following which they "climbed up the ladder from the Ant kiva, making their Emergence to the Third World." [51]

The transition to the fourth world is likewise an emergence, but it takes a different form. Destruction is now caused by the deluge, and the people are granted survival, each floating on the surface of the flood in a hollow reed. When summoned from the reeds they fashion boats from these, and travel from island to island (identified as the tops of the mountains of the third world), ultimately arriving at the fourth, and present, world. Sótuknang calls the islands "the footprints of your journey" and then causes them to disappear, one by one.[52] When all are gone he addresses the people, delineating the nature of the fourth world, and stating the purpose of migrations of the clans within it.

> "The name of this Fourth World is Túwaqachi, World Complete. You will find out why. It is not all beautiful and easy like the previous ones. It has height and depth, heat and cold, beauty and barrenness; it has everything for you to choose from. What you choose will determine if this time you can carry out the plan of Creation on it or whether it must in time be destroyed too. Now you will separate and go different ways to claim all the earth for the Creator. Each group of you will follow your own star until it stops. There you will settle. Now I must go. But you will have help from the proper deities, from your good spirits. Just keep your own doors open and always remember what I have told you. This is what I say." [53]

Sótuknang now disappears, and the clans are left to undertake their migrations in fulfillment of his instructions, ultimately each to be led to the same destination, the Hopi lands themselves, there to tell and retell the stories of their journeys, and to celebrate and reenact the emergences by which they have become "the *hopitu,* the peaceful ones." [54]

Of course much more is packed into the telling of the myths of the four worlds than we have been able to indicate in this brief focusing of the centrality of *emergence,* the thread binding them together. The four worlds are each given names:[55] *Tokpela* (Endless Space), *Tokpa* (Dark Midnight), *Kuskurza* ("an ancient term for which there is no modern meaning"),[56] and, as we have just seen, *Túwaqachi* (World Complete). And each world is assigned its direction (west, south, east, north, respectively) together with its symbolic color, bird, animal, mineral, and plant, all of which figure in the ceremonies derived from the myths.

One last point remains before we can leave the *Book of the Hopi.* The significance of the migrations cannot be overestimated, for these diverse wanderings of the clans of the tribe inform the sense of ultimacy with which the Hopi regard their lands. As Waters relays the unfolding of the year-long cycle of ceremonies it becomes clear that these wanderings join the myths in supplying the details of the rituals. To this is to be added a memorable insight that Waters drew from the elders who told him the stories comprising the book.

> At the conclusion of each major ceremony all the men who have taken part must remain in the kiva for another four days before returning to their families and fields. This retreat is an important part of the ceremony, for on the second day older men begin to relate the history of their clans and their migrations "so that we will always keep them deeply in our hearts. For the telling of our journeys is as much religious as the ceremonies themselves." [57]

Clearly, this telling of the journeys can make no sense apart from the lands regarded as sacred, in which the Hopi dwell.

The migrations have been completed. Despite the absolute impossibility of understanding the New Testament without coming to terms with the Old Testament (itself the yield of an emergence and wanderings) and the telling of the journeys of yet another set of tribes (the ancient Hebrews), the fact remains that the churches have yet to listen attentively to the stories of this—or of any—American Indian tribe. This is one of the reasons—in fact, the basic reason—why so many whites do not understand that to rob the red brothers and sisters of their lands is to rob them of their souls.

Nothing would be more fallacious or misleading than to suggest, or even to intimate, that in listening to Eastman, Black Elk (through Neihardt), and the Hopi (through Waters) we have heard all we need to hear, or all that can be heard. What we have done, however, is glimpse the trail that must be followed if we are to be able to grasp the contributions of red brothers and sisters to the theological pluralism so intrinsic to the American experience, and so long obstructed. The scope of the *Book of the Hopi* is more vast than that of *Black Elk Speaks,* and by comparison to Black Elk's vision the Hopi myths and legends are epic in articulation as well as intentionality. But just as we found to be the case with Black Elk's vision, so here with the Hopi stories, the building blocks of reflection are drawn from the world of nature, and the collective experiences of the tribe are understood in this framework, culminating in a collective self-understanding fixed in a given land. It is this hallowing of tribal lands that is the basic point in common in the religions of the tribes. In the light of this, other similarities, such as the predominance of the number *four* (the four ascents of Black Elk's vision, the four creation myths of the Hopi, the utilization of the four directions in the telling of visions and stories), achieve their significance.

All of this is the irrevocable background against which the American Indian religious thinker of today moves—whether he or she champions a return to the religions of the tribes, *or* yearns for the possibility of understanding and expressing the gospel of Jesus the Christ in Indian terms.

Only now, having attempted to rehearse something of the visions and the stories of the tribes, can we begin to grasp a fundamental clue to what would seem to be a basic characteristic of the American Indian temperament in all its myriad forms. This is the mark of self-effacing, soft-spoken humility. Eastman's portrayal of this is incisive.

> As a rule, the warrior who inspired the greatest terror in the hearts of his enemies was a man of the most exemplary gentleness, and almost feminine refinement, among his family and friends. A soft, low voice was considered an excellent thing in man, as well as in woman! Indeed, the enforced intimacy of tent life would soon become intolerable, were it not for these instinctive reserves and delicacies, this unfailing respect for the established place and possessions of every other member of the family circle, this habitual quiet, order and decorum.[58]

Clearly, the origins of this demeanor lie in part in practical necessity, but this is not enough to lay bare the deepest roots that yield it. Here, too, Eastman's formulation is memorable.

> The first American mingled with his pride a singular humility. Spiritual arrogance was foreign to his nature and teaching. He never claimed that the power of articulate speech was proof of superiority over the dumb creation; on the other hand, it is to him a perilous gift. He believes profoundly in silence—the sign of a perfect equilibrium. Silence is the absolute poise or balance of body, mind, and spirit. The man who preserves his selfhood ever calm and

unshaken by the storms of existence—not a leaf, as it were, astir on the tree; not a ripple upon the surface of shining pool—his, in the mind of the unlettered sage, is the ideal attitude and conduct of life.[59]

Speculative it may well be, but one can hardly fail to observe that this is, above all, one of the most misunderstood things about the red brother, and it is true of the red sister as well. When his self-control finally gives way to anger in the heat of struggle, the popular notion that attends the meaning of the word "savage" receives ample support in the manifestation of seething rage. But when he seeks to speak from the heart of his religious heritage, he can be expected to do so in a way that bears witness to the Great Mystery before which he stands. What is, then, in fact the sense of awe of the mystic may be mistaken for the indecisiveness of one whose prophetic intensity is shallow and weak. This is why the drastic differences in the *patterns* of relationship around the red/white/black triangle also involve, at the deepest levels, varying rates of relatability. We now have enough before us to attempt to come to terms with this.

B. *The Fluctuating Tempos of Plural Relationships*

One hazards the guess that it is true of all genuine pluralism that if the rates of relatability in such a context are constant, some one of the components, or some restricted combination of them, is still dominating all exchanges. We pointed to this when we first mentioned the parameter under consideration. Now, with the full ranges of the red/white/black triangle before us, the reality of this contention should be unavoidable.

The clue to the point is already present when one takes

up the question of the new emergence of red dignity. Red is not a subcategory of black. So we have heard Deloria cogently argue in explicating the fact that the issues that inform the passion for liberation on the part of red brothers and sisters are not coincidental with those at the heart of the Black Revolution. Such whites and blacks as hear this point have the task of understanding that the dominance of the black/white crisis can in itself simply leave intact the oppression that reds have always known. The tribal struggle involves the *land*, and that in a literal, fixed sense. For the red brothers and sisters the struggle for civil rights was, and remains, a road to the future only if it serves toward the redemption of their lands from the hands of the oppressors.

What we should now know is that this matter is infinitely deeper than it probably sounded at first. The complexity involved is not simply that of differing struggles for liberation, for to put the issue of liberation as the tribes must put it is to raise a religious question. It may well be one of the profound ironies of the American experience that the ignored heritages of the tribes of the first Americans may prove to be one of the decisive forces—perhaps *the* decisive force—that renders the intrinsically religious character of America's struggle beyond its long dying irrevocably explicit. This is not to say that many blacks and whites involved in the effort for a new tomorrow do not already feel that it has all the marks of ultimacy. But it is to recognize that not all blacks and whites in this struggle find their way into its turmoil in the light of faith. And whereas similar judgments are no doubt in order regarding some, perhaps many, of today's red men and women, the fact remains that the passion for the redemption of tribal lands simply cannot be divorced from its religious origins. Consequently, the inescapably religious character of the tensions around the red/white/black triangle, and the necessity of theologically informed efforts to transcend these tensions, come to the fore with unavoidable intensity.

To say this is to encounter the deepest levels of America's ethnic pluralism. The point can be put generally as follows: White slave masters so succeeded in dehistoricizing their black slaves that the route back to the latter's own tribal religions was virtually obliterated. This is not to say that these ancient forces left no marks on blacks in permanent diaspora, but it is to say that they are extremely difficult to discern. (Indeed, the real effort to discern them has gained momentum only since the Black Revolution.) The result is that America's black religious heritage is a composite of black genius plus channels of faith and expression derived from the dominant white culture's understanding of Christianity, so that the *theological* exchanges between blacks and whites are consistently couched in Christian terms.

The passion and intensity of these articulations remind one of the fervor of the Old Testament prophets, and of the New Testament successor to them, John the Baptist, in his pointing toward Jesus the Christ. In sharp contrast, and we should now be able to grasp this with some precision, the white invaders, despite their uniformly consistent ploy of the strategy of the broken word, did not succeed in obliterating the tribal religious heritage of America's red men and women. This heritage is present in the heart and soul of every contemporary American Indian religious thinker, whatever the purpose of his or her labors may be. New theological paths must be broken if these factors are to be given their due. For the religious heritage of America's whites *and* blacks is forever marked by the *prophetic* faith of the Biblical tradition, while that of the reds has an indelibly *mystical* hue. The long journey toward mutual intelligibility and mutual interdependence on the part of whites and blacks is a journey informed by the search for new prophetic creativity. When either, or both together, encounter red brothers and sisters committed to similar ends, the conversation shifts to the long-elusive goal of an authentic dialogue between prophets and mystics. The rates of relatability around the triangle thus vary—drastically. It is entirely possible to share the struggle for liberation and yet miss the real depths of the pluralism operative around the red/white/black triangle.

Here, by way of our own route, we arrive at the same set of concerns that seized, at the last, the imagination of one of the most insatiably curious theologians of our time, Paul Tillich. Given the modern world with its rapidly increasing intertwining of hitherto disparate cultures, it was inevitable that his attention would never rest until it had locked on the problematic of the history of religions. This would have to be the case, in the light of his long effort to develop the method of correlation, the attempt, that is, to juxtapose the urgent questions of our time with the answers that can be discerned in the faith. For Tillich, the endeavor "to correlate the questions implied in the situation with the answers implied in the message" [60] was a matter of rigorously disciplined balance. Neither message nor situation may be overemphasized. The message cannot be stated without having the situation in mind, because "the revelatory answer is meaningless if there is no question to which it is the answer. Man cannot receive an answer to a question he has not asked." [61] The situation, however, cannot dominate the correlation, for the message of faith is unique in its own right, and without this conviction, "theology would lose itself in the relativities of the 'situation'; it would become a 'situation' itself—for instance, the religious nationalism of the so-called German Christians and the religious progressivism of the so-called humanists in America." [62] Granted all this (and we touch briefly on matters which it took Tillich a lifetime of effort to clarify, culminating with his massive three-volume *Systematic Theology*), it is self-evident that such thinking is always open to the emergence of new problems. More than anything else, this accounts for the fact that Tillich was boldly moving toward new horizons when he died, and that whereas he had only a set of clues to offer those who, for whatever reasons, would come upon these same horizons, his insights leap alive for us.

During the last year of his life the problem of the relationship between Christianity and the non-Christian religions spun to the center of Tillich's reflections. It had never been absent from the purview of his thought, but neither had it occupied the central position in it. He was now beginning to ask what would happen if it did. A trip to Japan lay behind his Bampton Lectures at Columbia University in 1961. These were published in 1963 as *Christianity and the Encounter of the World Religions.* Then, during the winter and fall quarters of 1964 he shared (at his own suggestion) a seminar at the Divinity School of the University of Chicago with the celebrated historian of religions, Mircea Eliade.[63] A year later—specifically, on the evening of October 12, 1965—Tillich presented a public lecture entitled "The Significance of the History of Religions for the Systematic Theologian," on the occasion of a conference at the same school. It was literally his last address. At 4:00 A.M. the next morning he suffered a heart attack, and died ten days later. The lecture is remarkably comprehensive and precise, though confined to the scope of a single address.[64]

In moving across the ground of this last argument of Tillich's, it is important for us to know where its real uniqueness lies. Much of what he said has deep precedent, both within the discipline of the history of religions, and within the long discussion of his own *Systematic Theology*. But what Tillich was now insisting on was the intertwining of these two disciplines, and in so doing he was explicitly arguing *as a systematic theologian*. And whereas here too a long history could be adduced, running at least from Schleiermacher through Troeltsch, the fact remains that Tillich was breaking a new trail. What he could not have known, not because he was insensitive, but because the decisive events had yet to unfold, was that within the American scene itself a theological agenda was shaping which cannot even be approached, let alone executed, on any other basis than the one he attempted to describe. He or she who would deal *theologically* with America's ethnic revolutions must encounter the problematic of the history of religions. Tillich's suggestions offer one way, and so far the most compelling way, to go.

The introductory section of the lecture culminated with the rejection of two positions, the one typified by Barth, the other typified by the so-called "God is dead" theologians. Each of these are guilty of reductionism, Tillich argued, because "both are inclined to eliminate everything from Christianity except the figure of Jesus of Nazareth." [65] Neither, then, would be willing or competent to take up the critical issue Tillich sought to address, the clarification of the necessity of religion, or, to use his own memorable phraseology, the clarification of "the fact that spirit requires embodiment in order to become real and effective." [66] The attempt to do this took shape in the second broad cluster of ideas in the lecture, those in terms of which he sought to adumbrate "a theology of the history of religions." [67] Here, now, Tillich rejected the traditional approach to this question as being far too narrow: "The traditional view of the history of religions is limited to that history as it is told in the Old and New Testament, and enlarged to include church history as the continuity of that history. Other religions are not qualitatively distinguished from each other." [68] What is needed in place of this, he argued, is "a theology of the history of religions in which the positive valuation of universal revelation balances the initial valuation." [69] He characterized his approach to this effort as being "dynamic-typological." It involved three steps, the clarification of "the experience of the Holy," [70] and the clarification of each of the two inevitable critiques that eventuate from this experience. In taking up each of these we come to the nerve center of the lecture.

In setting out what he called his "tentative schema" for interpreting the religions, Tillich insisted that he was not arguing for a "progressive development," but was rather attempting to delineate "elements in the experience of the Holy which are always there if the Holy is experienced." [71] The first step was the delineation of the sacramental, the term Tillich used to refer to "the universal religious basis," namely, "the experience of the Holy within the finite." The formulation runs as follows:

> Universally in everything finite and particular, or in this and that finite, the Holy appears in a special way. I could call this the sacramental basis of all religions—the Holy here and now which can be seen, heard, dealt with, in spite of its mysterious character.[72]

Whenever, and wherever, and however the sacramental takes shape, two "critical movements" against its misuse, or "demonization," inexorably appear. The first of these is *the mystical*, and Tillich placed it alongside the sacramental as the second element in experience of the Holy:

> This mystical movement means that one is not satisfied with any of the concrete expressions of the Ultimate, of the Holy. One goes beyond them. Man goes to the one beyond any

manifoldness. The Holy as the Ultimate lies beyond any of
its embodiments.[73]

The second of these critical movements is *the ethical or
prophetic,* and this for him was the third element in the
experience of the Holy:

> Another element, or the third element in the religious
> experience, is the element of "ought to be." This is the
> ethical or prophetic element. Here the sacramental is
> criticized because of demonic consequences like the denial
> of justice in the name of holiness.[74]

With these three delineations before us we are in position
to grasp the goal of Tillich's efforts in this lecture. It was, of
course, the envisioning of the constructive unity of these
three elements. Here, above all, we must maintain our hold
on the fact that he spoke as a *systematic theologian.* But in
reiterating this we must be clear, as well, on the fact that he
was not just responding as a systematic theologian to the
thrust of the history of religions; he was, at the same time,
summoning this discipline into direct participation in the
tasks of systematic theology itself.

> I would like to describe the unity of these three elements in a
> religion which one could call—I hesitate to do so, but I don't
> know a better word—"The Religion of the Concrete Spirit."
> And it might well be that one can say the inner *telos,* which
> means the inner aim of a thing, such as the *telos* of the acorn
> is to become a tree—the inner aim of the history of religions
> is to become a Religion of the Concrete Spirit.[75]

Only now, as a full participant in the effort just conceived,
would he state his own Christian conviction. He pointed to
Pauline thought as exemplary of the goal he had defined,
and moved from this to a brief pondering of "an old symbol
for the Christ, Christus Victor," [76] as being due for new

reflection—reflection which would *both* articulate the specifically Christian contribution to the broader theological enterprise as now defined, *and* at the same time be liberated from the exclusivistic limitations that must no longer restrict the never-ending efforts to grasp Christology.

> [The Christus Victor symbol] points to the victory on the cross as a negation of any demonic claim. And I believe we see here immediately that this can give us a Christological approach which could liberate us from many of the dead ends into which the discussion of the Christological dogma has led the Christian churches from the very beginning.[77]

This drove Tillich to a truly daring suggestion regarding the significance of such a Christian contribution for the non-Christian religious worlds:

> The criterion for us as Christians is the event of the cross. That which has happened there in a symbolic way, which gives the criterion, also happens fragmentarily in other places, in other moments, has happened and will happen even though they are not historically or empirically connected with the cross.[78]

The third, and final, cluster of ideas of the lecture contained anything but mere addenda to the central points we have now set out for close inspection, for Tillich now sought, by way of concluding the address, to reflect on "the interpretation of the theological tradition in the light of religious phenomena." [79] On the basis of what he had now seen, he formed a new judgment of his own mighty effort in the *Systematic Theology*, noting carefully that it had been completed before the seminars he shared with Eliade, which yielded the new directions he was now exploring. In the light of these he now saw it as no longer sufficient. To be sure, it was the persistence with which he followed his own method of correlation that had driven him to the sighting of new horizons, but it was the same devotion to disciplined thought that informed his own indication of the limitations of his own central work. In setting it aside, he formulated the task for any such effort now.

> In terms of a kind of an apologia yet also a self-accusation, I must say that my own *Systematic Theology* was written before these seminars and had another intention, namely, the apologetic discussion against and with the secular. Its purpose was the discussion or the answering of questions coming from the scientific and philosophical criticism of Christianity. But perhaps we need a longer, more intensive period of interpenetration of systematic theological study and religious historical studies. Under such circumstances the structure of religious thought might develop in connection with another or different fragmentary manifestation of theonomy or of the Religion of the Concrete Spirit. This is my hope for the future of theology.[80]

This, then, cleared the way for the memorable depth of the peroration with which the address culminated:

> But now my last word. What does this mean for our relationship to the religion of which one is a theologian? Such a theology remains rooted in its experiential basis. Without this, no theology at all is possible. But it tries to formulate the basic experiences which are universally valid in universally valid statements. The universality of a religious statement does not lie in an all-embracing abstraction which would destroy religion as such, but it lies in the depths of every concrete religion. Above all it lies in the openness to spiritual freedom both from one's own foundation and for one's own foundation.[81]

The religion of concrete spirit is intrinsically plural, as plural as are the experiential bases of humanity's search for ultimacy. What Tillich envisioned was a conversation involving all *as peers* in this search, as over against the ancient hostilities that have always separated the manifold traditions. This is why openness to spiritual freedom, and not the all-embracing abstraction, is the only universal such a diverse unity can abide. This is also why the all-embracing abstraction was rejected, not as a viable but lesser alternative, but rather as the destructive enemy of religion itself. If this insight is put into operation, the result is the fluctuating tempos of the plural relationship that the religion of concrete spirit presupposes. Tillich saw this as he died. We have a chance to live it.

C. *The First Parameter of Reciprocal Creativity*

America itself provides a unique context within which to test and extend the theological logic of Tillich's last address. This he could not have known in the way that we must now know it; the Black Revolution had not yet replaced the civil rights movement, nor had the revolutions across the whole of America's ethnic spectrum that followed in its wake taken shape when he formulated new directions for theological reflection in the light of the seminar he shared with Eliade. A theology in red, white, and black is now both possible and necessary, and it is only the beginning step in this process of testing and extension. As we have now seen, if those from all sides of the red/white/black triangle participate in these new exchanges *as peers,* varying rates of relatability will be the order of the day. Only so will the exchanges themselves remain within the ferment of inexhaustibility. This is close to, if not identical with, Tillich's own point. The purpose of the final yield of his reflection is the facilitating of a new conversation, one nourished by the interpenetration of systematic theology and the history of religions, all in the name of that openness to spiritual freedom without which neither one's participation in the emergence of the religion of concrete spirit, nor one's free relationship to one's own foundation, can survive.

All of this we can borrow in our own attempt at precision. Mutual Intelligibility plus Mutual Interdependence yields Reciprocal Creativity—so we expressed where matters stood before we took into account the fact that the depth of the new emergence of red dignity is the religion of the land. With something of the religion of the land now before us we should be able to see that whereas white and black contributions to the new exchanges will move *to* the mystical critique of the sacramental *from* a prophetic base, red contributions will move in precisely the opposite direction. In this light we can embody the first parameter intrinsic to the equation in a single theorem:

> Theology in the context of ethnic pluralism is dependent upon sensitivity to the fact that the components of this pluralism relate to each other in varying rates, because this sensitivity is the precondition of the continuum of reciprocal creativity, and reciprocal creativity is the facilitator of spiritual freedom.

How far can this freedom go? How deeply can the creativity that emerges from the matrix of diversity penetrate? Here, as at the conclusion of the two preceding chapters, one thinks of ancient words from the origins of the faith, for one cannot wrestle with these issues as a Christian without hearing the echoes of the mighty argument of Paul in the Letter to the Galatians: "For freedom Christ has set us free; stand fast therefore, and do not submit again to a yoke of slavery" (Gal. 5:1). This freedom knows only one limit—the limit of love: "For you were called to freedom, brethren; only do not use your freedom as an opportunity for the flesh, but through love be servants of one another. For the whole law is fulfilled in one word, 'You shall love your neighbor as yourself' " (Gal. 5:13–14). How free is this freedom to love? Free enough to hear from a distance the yearning hope at the end of Black Elk's vision—and, hearing it, to hear the voices of his successors, both those who would understand the gospel anew and those who would return to the search of that old holy man?

5:
MUTUAL OPENNESS
TO CHANGE

Sensitivity to varying rates of relatability is the first parameter that must be operative if the combination of mutual intelligibility and mutual interdependence is to yield a continuum of reciprocal creativity. Alongside this is a second parameter, caught up in the phrase "mutual openness to change." Here again we must say that if this is not observed, all our prior efforts will be to no avail. Nothing healing—and obviously, then, nothing constructive—will have emerged unless all involved are willing to serve the goal of a tomorrow other than that implicit in the present as we know it. The only change that can be demanded is a change that is shared. All must be mutually open to it, and thus no one can monopolize it. Accordingly, while it is obvious, given the past, that no white has an automatic entrée to the task at hand, it must be clear that no black or red does either. The common recognition of this around the entirety of the red/white/black triangle is the essence of the second parameter. In a sense it does not lie simply "alongside" that sensitivity to the varying rates of relatability which this pluralism must manifest—it lies even deeper within the passion for reciprocal creativity, within the inner recesses of motive, aim, purpose. Moreover, its operation is so completely contemporary that it is difficult to discern. It is qualitative in character, just as is that openness to spiritual freedom of which we have heard Tillich speak, and it can only be seen in action.

Happily, there are voices now to be heard that exemplify this mutual openness to change, and they are the real tokens of the hope that a way toward a new tomorrow is beginning to develop. Here, though, we face a limitation that must be frankly acknowledged and willingly accepted. The reality of the second parameter is such that it can only be seen as one participates in the process it describes, and thus one can discern it only from the vantage point of one's own side of the triangle. From the white side of the triangle one can only hear and respond to black and red voices, with the hope that one's own speaking will be meaningful in the common enterprise. The white side of the triangle, then, will be heard from last, not so that the last word will be safely under control, but so that it will know its possible integrity only as one of several peers. When mutual openness to change is under consideration, a theology in red, white, and black cannot be talked about, it must be *done*—however fragmentary, of necessity, any single effort toward this end will be. Reciprocal creativity is an intrinsically collective enterprise.

A. *Black Theology: On the Way Toward Tomorrow Through the Recapturing of the Past*

In 1972 Gayraud S. Wilmore's *Black Religion and Black Radicalism* made its appearance. Wilmore stands within the inner circle of the most astute black theologians writing in America today. His work epitomizes both the rigor and the aggressive insights the black side of the red/white/black triangle places at the disposal of a possible new tomorrow.

The discussion unfolds a broad sweep of conclusions developed during a distinguished career as churchman, theologian, and civil rights leader. Now a professor at Colgate Rochester Divinity School, following two years as a professor at Boston University School of Theology, Wilmore brings to his teaching and writing a depth of experience that reached sharp focus over a nine-year period as chairman of the Division of Church and Race of the Board of National Missions of The United Presbyterian Church U.S.A. This experience involved the radicalizing and the redirecting of basic themes already sounded in his first book, *The Secular Relevance of the Church* (1962). He could not have known, when he completed this work, that the decade ahead would so relentlessly test his contention that the churches must recognize and use their own institutional power. With singular intensity the work now before us sets out the yield of that testing.

Wilmore's discussion constitutes the demonstration *par excellence* of the fact that black theology will find a new tomorrow only as it recaptures a past that has been distorted and suppressed. He marshals an impressive panorama of historical detail in developing his case, and does so in a way that assures the lasting significance of his work for all who would follow the theological paths we are exploring. At issue is an argument aimed at both white and black opposition.

> It is [the] radical thrust of Black people for human liberation expressed in theological terms and religious institutions which is the defining characteristic of Black Christianity and of Black religion in the United States, from the preacher-led slave revolts to the Black Manifesto of James Forman and the 1970 "Black Declaration of Independence" of the National Committee of Black Churchmen. . . .
>
> The radicals who deprecate the Black church, the Black

professionals who avoid it, and the Black television comedi-
ans who mimic it, need to know how facilely they have
absorbed the white man's ignorance and how they have
sewn themselves up in his bag. Black pride and power,
Black nationalism and Pan-Africanism have had no past
without the Black church and Black religion, and without
them it may well have no enduring future.[1]

Late in the book Wilmore discloses the schema that has in
fact ordered his discussion, and that will enable us to
analyze his argument as a whole. He contends that the
sources of black theology are threefold: (1) "the existing
Black community"; (2) "the writings and addresses of the
Black preachers and public men of the past"; and (3) "the
traditional religions of Africa." [2] For obvious reasons it is
with the third source that the book begins. The conclusion
Wilmore develops in connection with it then informs the
explication of the other two sources. The bulk of the
discussion is devoted to the treatment of the second source
of black theology, the tradition of black preachers and other
public men. Once this has been accomplished, Wilmore is
in a position to set out his understanding of the existing
black community, and the manner in which it now shapes
the theological task before today's black religious thinkers.

The decisive theme pervading Wilmore's discussion as a
whole is his insistence that black religion in America was,
and remains, a unique entity. With Troeltsch's labors in
mind we could say that what he demonstrates is its
historical individuality. What emerged was the product of
two forces—the "white Christianity" of Europe and America, and the lasting effects of African tribal religions. Both
of these were refracted by, and transmitted within, the
experience of slavery, in which they were blended. Wilmore says: "What we may call 'White Christianity' in
Europe and the United States has made a deep and lasting

impression upon Black people everywhere." At the same time he never tires of insisting that "Blacks have used Christianity not as it was delivered to them by segregated white churches, but as its truth was authenticated to them in the experience of suffering, to reinforce an ingrained religious temperament and to produce an indigenous religion oriented to freedom and human welfare." [3] Just *how* the traditional religions of Africa influenced, and were influenced by, this adaptation of Christianity is difficult if not impossible to reconstruct, as Wilmore concedes without hesitation.[4] But *that* this factor played a crucial role is beyond dispute in his judgment. Only so can he account for the fact that what emerged in the American black experience was a genuinely new phenomenon.

> For all its deficiencies and excesses, the religion that the slave practiced was his own. It was unmistakably the religion of an oppressed and segregated people. It had, of course, common features with white Protestantism and, in the French and Spanish areas, with Roman Catholicism. But it was forged not in the drawing rooms of the southern mansions, nor in the segregated balconies of the northern churches. It was born in Blackness. Its most direct antecedents were the quasi-religious, quasi-secular meetings which took place on the plantations, unimpeded by white supervision and under the inspired leadership of the first generation of African priests to be taken in slavery. It was soon suppressed and dominated by the religious instruction of the Society for the Propagation of the Gospel in Foreign Parts and the colonial churches—especially the Baptists and Methodists. But the faith that evolved from the coming together of diverse religious influences was a *tertium quid,* distinctly different from its two major contributors.[5]

The central burden of Wilmore's work is the exposition of the fact that American black religious creativity had, and has, an initiative of its own, rooted in ancient memory, tested, tortured, extended in the experience of slavery and the continuum of oppression still forced upon it, and struggling now to find and to state anew its own singular contribution to humanity's search for ultimacy. Intrinsic to this is the relentless demand: contemporary black theologians *must know* the labors of their forefathers, for if they do not, the uniqueness of their contributions cannot thrive. Precisely this demand is the point to Wilmore's prolonged treatment of the tradition of black preachers and other public men. He works out his exposition on the grand scale, and in the process he establishes an incisive claim:

> As white theology has its Augustine, its John Calvin, Martin Luther, Ulrich Zwingli, and John Wesley, Black theology has its Nat Turner, its Richard Allen, Martin Delany, Edward Blyden, and W. E. Burghardt Du Bois. Not all Black thinkers were ministers, but all of them were greatly influenced by Black religion. One cannot understand the genius of Black spirituality or the work of charismatic leaders like Martin King, Malcolm X or James Forman, without understanding how their interpretations of the Black experience were conditioned by great Black men of the past. Forman and Malcolm X belong as much to this theological tradition as [Adam Clayton] Powell or [Martin Luther] King.[6]

The fact is that neither the white nor the black communities have taken into the center of theological concern the findings of an inquiry such as Wilmore champions. The former has ignored them for convoluted reasons, including guilt and cultural myopia. The latter has made real beginnings along this line, but the revolution is still young, and countless studies such as Wilmore's are in order before it can be said that such insights inform the theological effort in a truly basic way. The explication of the tradition of the thought of black preachers and other public men leads Wilmore's readers across unfamiliar ground. To be sure, celebrated names, such as Denmark Vesey, Nat Turner, Martin Delany, and W. E. B. Du Bois, are there (and in the discussion of Turner, Wilmore is as devastating in his categorical rejection of Styron's portrait as we found Harding to be).[7] But there are also names not so well known. For example, one learns of David Walker (1785–1830), whose "Appeal to the Coloured Citizens of the World" (1829) Wilmore convincingly compares with Luther's "Open Letter to the Christian Nobility of the German Nation."[8] Or again, one hears of the Presbyterian minister, Edward Wilmot Blyden (b. 1832), whose writings "represent the most systematic development of the seminal Black theology which provided the intellectual substructure of Black Nationalism."[9] And one is called to come to terms with Bishop Henry McNeal Turner (b. 1834), of the African Methodist Episcopal Church, who "not only made a Black theology of liberation central to his preaching and writing, but also helped to implant the spirit of revolutionary religion in the independent churches of Africa which took up the struggle against colonialism and racism."[10] More than all that, one is immersed in an extremely informative recounting of the emergence of the National Committee of Black Churchmen in these recent years—an incomparable narrative, since Wilmore himself has been one of the key leaders in its development.

The conclusion toward which Wilmore's historical analysis drives is composite and processive in character, but it may be stated succinctly: The transmutation of the gospel of Jesus the Christ in the crucible of the black experience in America *was never completed,* and is *still under way.* To feel the forcefulness of Wilmore's argument we must note at least two basic components and an incisive question intrinsic to it.

The first component involves insight into the intentionality of that militancy that has always been so irrepressibly present in the black experience—namely, its yearning for a rapprochement between the races. By way of culminating his extended treatment of David Walker's "Appeal to the Coloured Citizens of the World" (1829) Wilmore articulates this as follows:

> As stridently militant as it is, Walker's Appeal does not represent unmitigated hostility and hatred of all white people. The spirit of the document strains toward some kind of resolution of the problem of race without violence—if white America will have it so. In that sense it is consonant with the dominant mood and motif of Black militance in the United States from the earliest slave petitions to the writings of Eldridge Cleaver.[11]

The second component involves insight into the persistence of a specifically Christian dimension within the heart of black militance, or, more carefully stated, within the heart of many of its significant exponents. Here a double-edged issue is in view. On the one hand, the point is increasingly perplexing, given the state of affairs now—so much so that many contemporary militant leaders either do not recognize it, or hold it in derision. On the other hand, the point is not to be taken as simply related causally to the yearning for reconciliation between the races, for Wilmore sees its compelling recurrence in vigorous champions of black nationalism, and not in those who would adjust to white dominance and oppression. The persistence of this Christian dimension Wilmore initially traces to historical necessity. Christianity filled the vacuum resulting from the dehistoricization of blacks at the hands of white overlords.

Commenting on the thought of Blyden and others he underscores this.

> Today when organized Christianity is in such disrepute among Black intellectuals because of its complicity in American imperialism and the oppression of nonwhite peoples, it will be difficult for some to understand the esteem in which radical protagonists of Black Nationalism like Blyden, Delany, Crummell, Garnet, Russwurm and many others held the Christian faith. It is, however, important to observe that, for all its defects, Christianity provided what was for these men the only familiar and coherent body of moral and ethical principles available for organizing and disciplining a distressed and chaotic people.[12]

Now whereas only a naïve Christian imperialism could claim that this body of moral and ethical principles is exclusively rooted in Christianity, the fact remains that the two are intertwined. This yields the trenchant question forced by Wilmore's discussion: Was the American black appropriation of Christianity simply the filling of a vacuum created by historical necessity? In saying that Wilmore's considered conclusion is that it was *not*, we must bear in mind his overarching contention that American black religion is a unique phenomenon, a genuine historical individuality. Only so can we perceive the real depths of a remark of Blyden's quoted by Wilmore, and the conjecture Wilmore builds upon it:

> "The lessons they have taught us," [Blyden] wrote in an exceptional encomium on American Protestantism, "from their uplifting effect upon thousands of the race, we have no doubt, contain the elements of imperishable truth, and make their appeal to some deep and inextinguishable consciousness of the soul." And it may be for this same reason that Black religion in America, thoughout its history, has remained essentially Christian and has attracted, until well

into the present century, the fidelity of some of the most militant and capable leaders of the race.[13]

Here now the rich yield of Wilmore's historical sensitivity emerges, and in dealing with it we actually move into his involvement in the last of his three sources of black theology, the "existing black community." The issue is simple: Will black religion in America remain "essentially Christian"? The urgency of the question is not minimal, and its answer is by no means self-evident. Above all, however, creativity in the face of this question necessitates untried theological moves. Two final steps will now take us to the summit of Wilmore's argument, his debate with James Cone, and his demonstration of the fact that neither the significance of Martin King nor that of Malcolm X may be grasped unless these two are understood together.

The first of these steps takes us onto perilous ground indeed, just as was the case when, following Deloria, we sought to take account of the tensions between red and black. All the same strictures apply here that were in order there, for in our time it may never be assumed that oppressors will not utilize contrasts such as we now must ponder for the perpetuation of oppression. Granted this, we may proceed, fully aware of the deeper fact that the contrast between Wilmore and Cone is not a hostile one. What emerges at Wilmore's hand drives Cone's radical points deeper, into terrain we have already seen Cone begin to explore in his third book, *The Spirituals and the Blues* (and it should be noted that Wilmore's manuscript was completed before this book appeared). Moreover, Wilmore's own appraisal of the significance of Cone's work is filled with praise. All of this intensifies, though, the forcefulness of the question he puts to Cone. The issue is simply this: How significant is the word "black" in the phrase "black theology"? In the light of what we have already heard Cone say it is hard to imagine that he could be superseded in this connection. This, however, is precisely what happens.

What bothers Wilmore is Cone's willingness to construe blackness as an *ontological symbol* describing the meaning of oppression in America, and embracing all who identify with, and participate in, the struggle against it. For Wilmore, this is a fatal concession, though he well appreciates what Cone attempted with this conceptualization, and why he proposed it. According to Wilmore's account, Cone "was the first to suggest the broad outlines of a Black theology based upon an essentially classical interpretation of the Christian faith." [14] As a consequence, he became the target of those who argued that "Blackness is an illegitimate basis for a Christian theology," and that "there is nothing in the historical experience of Black people that justifies the particularity of the claim that the whole of Biblical revelation points to what is being called Black theology." [15] The idea of blackness as an ontological symbol provided Cone with a way beyond this critique, and—as we noted when we first touched upon it—did so without undermining the cogency of his polemic.[16] As Wilmore sees it, this became Cone's way of stating the universal significance of black theology.[17] The trouble is that such a move threatens the uniqueness of the black religious experience in America, and because of the comprehensive historical discussion out of which Wilmore's constructive efforts move he is not willing to make this sacrifice. Wilmore's formulation of this is one of the most memorable passages in his book:

> To say that being Black in America has little to do with skin color is, at best, only half true. It is possible to argue that in a world dominated by white power that has been inextrica-

ble from white Christianity, being Black, or identifiably "Negroid," is a unique experience and has produced a unique religion, closely related to, but not exclusively bound by, the Christian tradition. Simply being oppressed or psychologically and politically in sympathy with the dispossessed does not deliver one into the experience of Blackness any more than putting on a blindfold delivers one into the experience of being blind.[18]

To see this is to arrive at the center of Wilmore's critical response to Cone's version of black theology. We have argued that Cone's use of the usual list of white theological giants is understandable given the polemical task with which he has been mainly preoccupied. Wilmore, however, will not allow us to leave the matter there. Like Cone, he sees a universal significance to the contribution that black theology must construct, and like Cone, he identifies this contribution with the explication of liberation. But unlike Cone he refuses to work this out within the confines of "the norms of white systematic theology." [19] Hence the searching question he puts to Cone, and to all who would take seriously the history he has tried to explicate:

> Is Black theology simply the Blackenization of the whole spectrum of traditional Christian theology, with particular emphasis upon the liberation of the oppressed, or does it find in the experience of the oppression of Black people, as *black*, a singular religiosity, identified not only with Christianity, but with other religions as well? [20]

How significant is the word "black" in the phrase "black theology"? For Wilmore its significance is that of a pointer to a reality that is intrinsic to a unique experience—one that must be stated in terms of its own indigenous insights. He is persuaded that there is no other route to the discerning of the universal implications of the black religious experience in America.

> Black theology's contribution to the universal knowledge of God does not lie in its being only the reverse side of traditional Christian theology—white theology in Black vesture. . . . Rather, in its illumination of the religious meaning of Black liberation, Black theology breaks with the determinative norms of white theology and unveils the deepest meaning of human freedom for all men.[21]

Wilmore is willing to abide by the regimen informing his critique of Cone. This is clearly evident in his insistence that Martin King and Malcolm X be understood together— an insistence that we are designating the second, and last, step to the summit of his argument. His case turns on the point we have had before us all along, namely, the contention that black religion in America is a discrete historical individuality. His claim is that in the existing black community "the tradition of Black folk religion is still extant and continues to stand over against the institutional church."[22] This tradition knows its own vitality, now merging with the black church, now departing from it, but always vibrant in "providing the resources for radical movements in the Black community,"[23] and always observable in a process of ebbing and flowing, in Wilmore's way of putting it. The proper subject of black theological reflection, so he argues, is precisely the dynamic thus isolated.

> This spirit is still the soul of Black religion and Black culture. Black theology must begin to understand and interpret it before it turns to white theologians for the substance of its reflection. The ebb and flow of Black folk religion is a constituent factor in every important crisis and development in the Black community. When the community is relatively integrated with the white society it recedes from Black institutions to form a hard core of unassimilable Black nationalism in an obscure corner of the social system—biding its time. When the community is hard-pressed, when

hopes fade and the glimmer of light at the end of the tunnel is blocked out by resurgent white racism, then the essential folk element in Black religion exhibits itself again and begins anew to infiltrate the institutions which had neglected it. That is the meaning of the religion of Black Power today and the renewal of a radical Black theology within the contemporary Black church.[24]

This passage is the clue to Wilmore's juxtaposition of Martin King and Malcolm X. He is not the first to insist that they be thought of together,[25] but his bold attempt to do so *theologically* places his treatment among the most incisive yet to appear.

As Wilmore reads King, the most ingenious thing about his charisma was his ability to articulate his insights, grounded in the most cerebral kind of study, in the context of the religious spirit intrinsic to the black community. "The real power of his southern campaign lay in his ability to combine dexterously a simplistic but highly sophisticated philosophy and tactic with the folk religion and revival technique of the Black Baptist preacher." [26] But however adroitly one takes apart the components of King's reflection and witness, the question of the reception of his labors defies any uncomplicated appraisal. Wilmore argues that two points must be seen in this connection. On the one hand, the reaction of the black church to King's efforts was anything but uniform and positive.

It must be acknowledged that the Black church in its national institutional form, almost as much as the white church, was more of a spectator than a participant in the events which marked the progress of the civil rights movement under SCLC [Southern Christian Leadership Conference], SNCC [Student Non-Violent Coordinating Committee] and CORE [Congress of Racial Equality].[27]

On the other hand, the very thing that made King effective, precisely his sensitivity to the complex religious spirit of the black community, put him in touch with dynamics he could not control. From this perspective Wilmore makes good his claim that King's labors were causally related to the rise of the Black Revolution. In so doing he brings out the fact that the dynamics of black nationalism, which King could not avoid encountering, included not only figures with whom we have watched him debate, but also those whose religious insights ran in directions opposite his own.

> Martin King, for all of his boisterous detractors, ushered in the idea of Black Power by making Black Americans conscious of their power to change the world. He could not sustain the dominance of Black Christian tradition, and before his assassination . . . he was obliged to share the leadership of the masses with the aggressive secularity of Stokely Carmichael and H. Rap Brown. But more significant for Black Power and the dechristianization of Black radicalism was another son of a Baptist preacher, Malcolm X.[28]

Malcolm X became the best known, and surely was the most effective, Black Muslim spokesman of his time. He had been attracted by, and then became totally committed to, Elijah Muhammad's Nation of Islam while serving a long prison sentence for burglary (in the state prison at Charlestown, Massachusetts). The religion that touched and so profoundly altered the life of Malcolm X offered him both a clue to the understanding of the degradation through which he had come, and a mission that dominated his subsequent creativity. What emerged from prison was a brilliant, self-taught, militantly religious intellectual, for, motivated by the conviction that now seized his imagination, he became (and continued to be) an insatiable reader. There then unfolded the tortuous career of a radical religious spokesman for the cause of black liberation. The astonishing story of this transformation is set out in detail in *The Autobiography of Malcolm X*, on which Malcolm collaborated with Alex Haley, and which was completed in 1964, within a year of his death. The work is one of the truly great documents of the Black Revolution, and it is unforgettably moving for all who read it with care.

It was this self-made scholar who fixed with precision the polemical line of the Black Muslims against the black church.[29] This is reflected in his earliest address at Temple Number One of the Nation of Islam, in Detroit, Michigan, where Malcolm's career as a Black Muslim minister began. Haley sets out Malcolm's recollection of the core of this sermon in the *Autobiography* as follows (and following Wilmore's lead we will take it as the clue to Malcolm's labors as a whole):

> My brothers and sisters, our white slavemaster's Christian religion has taught us black people here in the wilderness of North America that we will sprout wings when we die and fly up into the sky where God will have for us a special place called heaven. This is white man's Christian religion used to *brainwash* us black people! We have *accepted* it! We have *embraced* it! We have *believed* it! We have *practiced* it! And while we are doing all of that, for himself, this blue-eyed devil has *twisted* his Christianity, to keep his *foot* on our backs . . . to keep our eyes fixed on the pie in the sky and heaven in the hereafter . . . while *he* enjoys *his* heaven right *here* . . . on *this earth* . . . in *this life*.[30]

Ultimately Malcolm moved beyond the Nation of Islam, this being the outcome of his break with Elijah Muhammad, and this move led to the widening of his horizons with his pilgrimage to Mecca in the spring of 1964. The transition into the realm of orthodox Islam generated a memorable deepening and broadening of his understanding of white humanity. (In this connection the pivotal evidence is his letter from Mecca and his own interpretation of this letter[31] upon his return.) But this did *not* mean a relaxation of his radical opposition to the distortion of Christianity at the hands of white America. The point to his founding of the Muslim Mosque, Inc., and the Organization of Afro-American Unity was the effort to establish a real relation between the black religious spirit and the real Islam, and to internationalize the struggle for the liberation of black America. That these factors together led to his assassination on February 21, 1965, is clear; *how* they did so will never be known.

Wilmore's appraisal of the significance of Malcolm X is consistent with the argument of his book as a whole, and, more than that, it opens the way for the most constructive and far-reaching of his contributions to a theology in red, white, and black. Basic to all this is Wilmore's insistence that Malcolm X was "one of the great prophets of Black liberation," and that this can be grasped only "if one understands the meaning of religion in the Black experience." [32] Without hesitation Wilmore formulates the radical conclusion that his comprehensive inquiry forces:

> The legacy of Malcolm cannot be the exclusive possession of any one group. . . . Although he repudiated Christianity, his prophetic ministry as a Black Muslim contributed to the further development of that indigenous Black religion which was never exclusively Christian in the historic sense. And what he stood for as an exponent of that ghettoized Black religion—namely, justice and liberation—was the continuation of a great tradition of nativistic-messianic religion in the United States, Africa and the Caribbean. Whatever else Black Christianity may be, it is also a part of the tradition he shared, and it is precisely for this reason that many Black churchmen are saying today, "The God who spoke by the

prophets and in the fullness of time by his Son, *now in this present time, speaks to us through Brother Malcolm.*" [33]

Wilmore here refers the reader to his 1969 article, "The Black Church in Search of a New Theology." [34] He knows what it means to contend as churchman and theologian with the impact of Malcolm X on the black church and the black community. But he knows more than this. He knows the decisive questions that emerge from the necessary juxtaposition of this figure with Martin King.

> What could have been a more radical understanding of Black America than Malcolm's when he called for Black people to give up the "slave religion" of Christianity and discover integrity and brotherhood in the Nation of Islam? . . . And what could have been more radical than Martin's daring belief that in twentieth-century America—after two world wars, a devastating economic depression, and a series of ill-advised imperialistic adventures in Latin America and Southeast Asia—it was possible to make white people Christians, to make love the operative agent of reconciliation between Black and white, rich and poor? [35]

How deeply Martin and Malcolm recognized their interdependence on, as well as their independence from, each other must always remain an open question—though there is a fascinating indication that a relationship was beginning, with Malcolm's visit to Selma, Alabama, within days of his death, as the crisis there moved toward its culmination.[36] What is beyond doubt, however, is that the fact that they must be understood together demands genuinely new theological construction.

> The radical faiths of Malcolm and Martin coalesce in the opaque depths of a Black spirituality that is neither Protestant nor Catholic, Christian nor Islamic in its essence, but both comprehends and transcends these ways of believing in

God by experiencing his real presence, by becoming one
with him in suffering, in struggle and in the celebration of
the liberation of man.[37]

Wilmore's argument as a whole is now before us. To
explore it is to behold the fact that black theology is on the
road to tomorrow by way of recapturing the past. More
than the record of suffering has been encountered in this
effort to recapitulate the unfolding of the black religious
spirit in the context of the American black experience, and
for that reason more than polemics and rhetoric has been
heard. What has been encountered—to follow Tillich's
lead—is the emergence of a religion of concrete spirit, and
what has been heard is a voice of new stature and new
creativity, evoked by the revolutionary resistance to the
distortion and suppression of this spirit. The process which
we have already seen to be operative in the movement of
James Cone's thought has been drastically intensified by the
breadth and detail of Wilmore's constructive analysis.
Consequently, the question that emerged from following
Cone's argument now recurs with greater forcefulness. In
its refined form that question was: Is there a depth to which
the partisan theology of the oppressed points, one that will
continue to assert itself when oppression is eradicated? [38]
This same question must now be put to Wilmore, and the
answer to it illuminates the sense in which he is exemplary
of that *mutual openness to change* without which the dream
of reciprocal creativity will remain only a haunting indication of what tomorrow could, and should, be.

In our discussion of Cone's thought we reached the
conclusion that the depth that will continue to assert itself
even if oppression truly disappears is a new reality, the
reality of the experience and promise of the liberated.[39]
What was an unavoidable possibility in reflecting on Cone's

argument becomes an incontrovertible conclusion when Wilmore's discussion is taken into account. For Wilmore's argument demonstrates the fact that theological reflection on this side of the Black Revolution must now regard as of major significance an experience which it has, until now, left on the edges of its concerns. Wilmore's refusal to buy Cone's understanding of blackness as an ontological symbol embracing all who join the struggle for liberation forces the full implication of this contention into the open. To recapture the past as Wilmore has done is to bring into being a new reality. Only one who knows the black experience from within can formulate the intrinsic interconnection between the theological significance of Martin King and that of Malcolm X. And this is so because only one who shares the black experience from within knows the absolute necessity of so doing. For a black theologian, the clarification of the meaning of this interconnection has priority over the task of fitting ideas into the sweep of the tradition of white theological reflection. One can deny this only at the peril of omitting vast segments of the terrain of the black religious spirit. One can accept it only at the risk of charting a new agenda for theological labor. And those from outside can respond to it only by negotiating with it *on a par.* New history demands new theological construction. This is the burden of the conclusion that Wilmore forges in the light of his juxtaposition of Martin and Malcolm. He is open to the rigorous demands of the task that it entails.

Is he open to more than this? Is he open to a conversation beyond the realm of the complex religious spirit that has shaped him? Everything turns on what he means by the claim that black theology, in its explication of the liberation of blacks, in fact speaks to the question of the freedom of *all* humanity. If Wilmore is correct in this claim, the testing and the embodiment of this conclusion necessarily involves more than liberated black people. The white insights of those who were oppressors must be added to the insights of those who have resisted oppression before this claim can be made good, as must the red insights of those who have shared the struggle against oppression and won their own victory over it. Ultimately the entire mosaic that is humanity must be involved. Only so can black theology's "contribution to the universal knowledge of God" be truly stated in terms of "the deepest meaning of freedom for all men." [40] Only if all humanity is involved can the unforgettable heritage of black suffering bear on the freedom of all humanity, and on its search for liberating ultimacy. Wilmore exemplifies the quality described by the parameter of *mutual openness to change* because his own argument envisions a world that cannot be real without it.

B. *Red Theology: The Time of Transition*

The precondition of hearing the red brothers and sisters make their contribution to a present and future theology in red, white, and black is the recognition of the bi-religious character of all American Indians. The time of transition to which we have heard Charles Eastman make reference[41] is still upon them, and upon us, and no meaningful understanding of where today's red thinkers are going can ever take shape without laying hold of this fact. The continuation of outrage among the tribes is rooted in this nexus, for the failure of the non-Indian world to grasp these dynamics accounts for the prevailing restriction of the red world to the realm of interesting anachronisms. Hence, struggle remains the order of the day—struggle to gain time and room for new self-understanding to emerge. On this side of the centuries-long attempt to Christianize the tribes the struggle for liberation from oppression takes one of two vectors—either a return to the tribal religions of the past in order then to bring these into the present as guides to tomorrow, or the insistence on reaching an understanding of Christianity that is indigenous to the tribal world itself. These two vectors have been long in shaping. In these very present years they have emerged with great forcefulness. But in either case what is happening is the unfolding of new thought—either a *new* tribalism, a trans-tribal tribalism, so to speak, or a new Christianity, one that celebrates its discovery of an Indian version of the ancient gospel of Jesus the Christ. Moreover, whereas it is true that long traditions stand behind each of these developments there are, nevertheless, radically new departures involved in each of them, so that in a profound sense it is only the beginning stages of each of them that we can point to now. And the enigmatic thing—the thing that is so fascinating and stimulating for all with ears to hear, Indians and non-Indians alike—is that despite initial impressions these two options are not in opposition, but are, in fact, blended. For what is unfolding before our eyes in our own time is, in Tillich's sense, a new religion of concrete spirit.

The fourth book from the hand of Vine Deloria, Jr., *God Is Red*, made its appearance in the fall of 1973. In this work Deloria's demand for admittance as a peer into the theological conversations of the present—a demand we have already discerned in his earlier works—receives its most forceful articulation, since now we have not only a new specification of the bill of particulars with which he rightly indicts the oppressors of all Indians, we also have the first detailed formulations of his contributions to theology in the context of ethnic pluralism. The updating of the indictment is important in its own right, including as it does a relentless delineation of Indian outrage over the increasingly recurrent desecration of burial grounds[42] and incisive appraisals both of the (fall 1972) militant occupation of the Washington offices of the Bureau of Indian Affairs[43] and of the (winter 1973) revisitation of tragedy and violence at Wounded Knee.[44] What must now occupy our attention, however, is the outlining of Deloria's theological argument, for it is as a religious thinker, not as an antiquarian, and not as a reporter, that he labors, and it is only on the front of theological exchange that his work can be properly appraised with the respect that is so clearly his due.

We have already taken note of one of the most basic elements of Deloria's theological struggle. This is his refusal of the confines suggested by the multiplicity of the tribes.[45] For the red religious thinker this is an absolutely necessary move. To be sure, no such thinker can be expected to renounce the tribal tradition he or she knows best, that of his or her own tribe. But neither will such a person remain completely within that tradition. The demands of the context are demands for *new* construction, and, in the face of these demands, to accept being limited to the explication of yesterday's realities and insights would be to abdicate responsibility in the context of today's necessity. Having said this, we must insist at the same time that Deloria can only be understood as a tribal thinker whose sense of identity is his most cherished asset. But as we shall see, he does not seek to systematize and codify the insights of as many tribes as possible; he seeks rather to think in the present as one whose perspective is that of tribal humanity. Hence our awkward but necessary phrase—Deloria is not a pan-tribal thinker; he is a trans-tribal thinker who remains tribal in outlook and insight, so that what he attempts is the theology of trans-tribal tribalism. It is a work very much in process, of course, but already we can discern several key features, and a decisive problem.

That what we have just described is what actually takes

place in *God Is Red* is clearly indicated by the initial formulation of the questions with which Deloria is preoccupied in this book. Once the updating of the indictment has been unfolded he sets out these questions as follows:

> Can we survive increasing speed and constant migration and hold the same religious convictions about the world that men held two centuries ago? Or that they held even a century ago? Or in the previous decade? [46]

Now particularly because the polemical dimension of Deloria's efforts is a dominant characteristic of all that he says in this work, it is necessary to note the observation that immediately follows the formulation of these lead questions. Deloria takes them to be questions before *all* religions. Without doubt, his openness to change is rooted in his sensitivity to the *permanence* of the ethnic pluralism that constitutes the American scene. No careful reading of his work as a whole, and certainly no close reading of *God Is Red*, can overlook this basic assumption.

> Almost everywhere we turn whether we be red, white, black, brown, or yellow, we are confronted with the necessity of renewing our vision of the totality of our existence, our understanding of the nature of the universe, and the paths by which we can move forward as diverse peoples upon the continent. At no point, however, have we dug sufficiently into the nature of the problems we face to tear ourselves away from traditional assumptions and find a place to stand from which we can view the breadth and depth of the task.[47]

Two factors inform Deloria's rejection of Christianity—its impotence in the face of the ecological crisis, and its myopic imperialism, rooted in the absolutizing of its own history. The genius of his point is that these two factors are intertwined. The incompetence of Christianity in the face of the problem of the impending environmental disaster—an incompetence which, it must be admitted, is not restricted to the Christianity that Deloria has known and experiences—has to do with the fact that no simple reformulation of its long-held convictions will now suffice, since all this can yield is new ethical intensification. The urgency of the problem at hand demands more than just new ethics, it demands new thought, thought in a style that Christianity has always been suspicious of, and usually has rejected.

> Attempting to shift the American/Western/Christian outlook from a preoccupation with a particular history and the great concern with time to an examination of spaces, places, and lands requires more than the relatively simple admission of guilt before ecological gurus. Rather a total reorientation as to the impact of viewing life in different categories must be established.[48]

Deloria, of course, is hardly the first to call for new thought. There is, however, a unique twist to his version of this perennial plea. What is at stake is not "a redefinition of spaces and places in terms of temporal concepts, but rather a relinquishment of temporal attitudes altogether. . . ." [49] This is the juncture at which his effort to bring forward a trans-tribal theological contribution gains its cogency. In the present arena of urgency the heirs of the religion of the land have things to say that are indispensable for the emergence of the new thought that we all must have.

In taking his stand, Deloria knows full well that a rigorous demand is being made on *all* ancient, time-honored, religious certainties. Christianity's preoccupation with its own history, and the lack of a sense of history in the tribes, must both be confronted, and in each case the confrontation is shot through with complexity. The former is easier to see.

As over against it an intensity of polemical caricature informs Deloria's assault.[50] But the real force of his relentless critique will be recognized only when one sees that his rage is aimed at an imperialism that now stands irrevocably exposed, in such a way that neither its intrinsic immorality *nor the defects of its thought* can be denied any longer.

> Christian religion and the Western idea of history are inseparable and mutually self-supporting. To retrench the traditional concept of Western history at this point would mean to invalidate the justifications for conquering the Western Hemisphere. Americans in some manner will cling to the traditional idea that they suddenly came upon a vacant land on which they created the world's most affluent society. Not only is such an idea false, it is absurd. Yet without it both Western man and his religion stand naked before the world.[51]

For Deloria even this does not in itself disclose the heart of the problem, for the real issue lies in the fact that, as he understands it, Christian theological erudition today is pervaded by a reluctance to assert categorically the actualities in which it is rooted. It seems, from his point of view, always to back off from the question as to whether it is rooted in something that *happened.* The thrust of his argument becomes clear in a remarkable chapter entitled "The Spatial Problem of History," and it has to do with the real center of his contention against Christianity—a contention which is not simply restricted to the ecological problem or even the question of cultural imperialism, but involves the nature of religious experience itself. For Deloria, given his orientation to space, not time, religion has to do with facts, not symbols.

> This dilemma over the nature of history occurs and will occur whenever a religion is divorced from space and made

an exclusive agent of time. Events become symbolic teaching devices, and the actual sequence of physical action which could indicate a divine intervention becomes unimportant; what is important are the moral lessons and ethical choices the legend illustrates.[52]

In sharp contrast to this is the literalism of the tribes, entailing a certainty that is always present when space, not time, has the upper hand.

The contrast between Christianity and its interpretation of history—the temporal dimension—and the American Indian tribal religions—basically spatially located—is clearly illustrated when we understand the nature of sacred mountains, sacred hills, sacred rivers, and other geographical features sacred to Indian tribes. The Navajo, for example, have sacred mountains where they believe that they rose from the underworld. Now there is no doubt in any Navajo's mind that these particular mountains are the exact mountains where it all took place. There is no beating around the bush on that. No one can say when the creation story of the Navajo happened, but everyone is fairly certain where the emergence took place.[53]

The point at hand is far more sophisticated than it is likely to appear to hasty readers. Deloria is not insisting on a false certainty. He is no more an idolator than his Christian counterparts in the world of the tribes. Nor is he championing a simplistic attack on the inevitability of symbolization in religion. What he is asserting is the fact that *place*, not time alone, has a decisive role to play in the shaping of religious symbols, and that since this is so, any attempt at *universal* symbols must be challenged.

What students of religion have failed to recognize is the unique nature of religious symbolism, its apparent correspondence with land masses, its vibrant ability to reassert itself in times of spiritual crisis, and the absence of a universal symbol system of religious experience.[54]

The "clashing of religions," so Deloria argues, is not simply a matter of "differentials on a time scale of social evolution"; what is in order is a "careful examination" of "the nature of disagreements and the origin of these differences in both the religious and geographical dimension of men's lives." [55]

Here, now, the heart of Deloria's constructive efforts comes into view. As we have noted, his thought confronts not only Christianity but the religion of the tribes. He is restive under restrictions from either source, however. Whereas he charges Christianity with the error of absolutizing its own history, he admits that the lack of a sense of history inhibits the development of new contributions from the side of the tribes. These two points are conjoined.

> If the lack of a sense of history can be called a shortcoming of tribal religions, as indeed it can, overemphasis on historic reality and its attendant consequences can certainly be called a bad grade for the Christian religion.[56]

Deloria's own efforts to move beyond this limitation of the tribal perspective, while at the same time maintaining a running fire against Christianity, pivots on what at first glance has all the marks of an irrational notion. This is his partisan elaboration of the ideas—bizarre to most—of Immanuel Velikovsky, psychoanalyst turned astronomer, who claims to have demonstrated conclusively the past occurrence of an astronomical cataclysm that accounts for the emergence of the world religions. So, at any rate, Deloria reads him,[57] and this reading serves his case well, for in supposing that Velikovsky is correct,[58] he is able to contend that not only the Hebrew exodus is explained, but also the intrinsically varied religious developments in other parts of the world. Moreover, this opens the way for the assertion of a real possibility, the possibility that the memory of the tribes is more comprehensive than that of the West.

> Suppose we find in the tribal traditions a memory that is not only more correct in many aspects than that of the Western religions, but suppose that we find in them the longer and more extensive history of mankind. That prospect has rarely been considered by Westerners. Yet it is precisely the consideration that must be made, if Western men are to be released from their religiously ethnocentric universe.[59]

The trouble is that Deloria, by the vigor with which he explicates and defends Velikovsky, risks being rejected on this ground alone. This would be tragic, for such a rejection would be able to sidestep both the questions and the insights Deloria has developed to date, none of which are dependent upon Velikovsky's suggestions. Even if the latter were proved to be not a genius but a charlatan, the question we have just seen Deloria pose remains with all its intensity, and will continue to do so as long as the identity of the tribes remains impervious to genocidal assaults, as it has now done for centuries. For the fact is that the symbols of any religious tradition are deeply rooted in the land of their origin, and the unfolding depths of meaning that such symbols are capable of generating can be discerned only in terms of the history that involves that land itself. The transcending of the limits of that given space can never cancel out what Deloria incisively calls (as we have already noted) "The Spatial Problem of History." [60]

To see this is to cross the threshold of Deloria's confrontation of the tribes. His work is a summons to the tribes into the effort at what we have called a trans-tribal tribal theology. This summons to *new tribal thought* is informed by a sense of urgency that is anything but naïve. Indeed, it has the mark of authenticity that is manifest in any such summons to genuinely new tasks—it knows that the effort can fail. To insist, as Deloria does, that Indians must struggle to see to it that "their religion is taken seriously as a religion" is to know that "an almost total translation of tribal beliefs into contemporary terms must be accomplished today by Indians of this generation." [61] Such a labor must also know that all that is certain about the future is that it entails a time of testing.

> The primary thesis of tribal religions, the relationship of a particular people with a particular land, and the belief of many tribal religions that certain places have special sacred significance must itself be tested in the years ahead. Young Indians must once again take up the vision quests, the search of revelations and dreams, and the responsibility to make the tribal community come alive as a community even with the tremendous hurdles that exist in the modern world. [62]

Red theology is in transition—a transition that is rooted in the *bi-religious* character of all red thought today. Deloria's labors provide a remarkable demonstration of this. As we saw in introducing him to our discussion, his background is *both* tribal *and* Christian. [63] The fact that the work now before us is written by one who has deeply absorbed *both* traditions yields the double-edged significance of his insights. In the very process of renouncing Christianity and moving *ahead* to a new religion of the tribes he does more than confront the tribes with the demand for new thought; he confronts Christianity as well with this same trail to the future. No sensitive Christian, whatever his or her identity, can fail to hear the immensely positive and constructive challenge in the following words:

> Christianity itself may find the strength to survive, if it honestly faces the necessity to surrender its narrow interpre-

tation of history and embark on a determined search for the true meaning of man's life on this planet. Even surrendering a belief in a god who exercises supremacy over world events becomes possible, if in surrendering the belief, one comes to a greater understanding of the nature of religion and religious experiences. For a divinity, if indeed one exists, cannot even be bound in doctrines and beliefs in any ultimate sense. To restrict one's god then to a particular mode of operation and sequence of appearance would seem to be irreligious and the utmost folly.[64]

To respond to this challenge is to know that it can be dealt with only by a theology in red, white, and black—a theology that itself yearns for the full mosaic that is humanity, one that one day will be a theology in red, white, black, brown, and yellow. Such a theology understands that more than skillful writing informs the beauty of the fact that the title of Deloria's book comes from its closing lines, for such a theology will have learned that the symbols from the religions of other lands must make peace with those encountered here.

Who will find peace with the lands? The future of mankind lies waiting for those who will come to understand their lives and take up their responsibilities to all living things. Who will listen to the trees, the animals and birds, the voices of the places of the land? As the long-forgotten peoples of the respective continents rise and begin to reclaim their ancient heritage, they will discover the meaning of the lands of their ancestors. That is when the invaders of the North American continent will finally discover that for this land, God is Red.[65]

Precisely how is it that Deloria's labors exemplify red theology in transition? This is the fascinating problem we must come to terms with before we are in touch with the depths of his creativity, and with something of the contours of his thought now before us we are in a position to take its measure. We have contended that his thought is bi-religious. We can see what it means to say this by noting a decisive contrast. On the one hand we must comment on a fact that can be simply stated, but that has immense implications. Deloria's theological position can be *argued.* His book *God Is Red* (indeed his writing as a whole) does not consist of the retelling of the stories that enshrine the red religion of the land, nor even of the creation of new stories that could do so. In sharp contrast to him, in this regard, one could bring to mind *Seven Arrows* (Harper & Row, 1972), the beautiful and powerful work of the contemporary Cheyenne writer, Hyemeyohsts Storm. If one wants to know how to teach the heritage of a tribe when one's only library is nature, one's only requisite competence is imagination, one's only passion is the gripping symbolism of an inexhaustible narrative, then Storm's *Seven Arrows* is the source to consult.[66]

Now the point is that Deloria's work is not cast in this form. Whereas his substantive agreement with Storm's concerns is conclusively demonstrable, the *formal* difference between his work and Storm's would have to be measured in miles. Storm, like Deloria, seeks to place the thought world of the tribes before his readers, but he does so in a way that evokes *response,* not *debate.* Were we to proceed to a close analysis of *Seven Arrows* at this point we would duplicate the task already attempted in our treatment of Black Elk's vision and the Hopi creation stories, not because Storm seeks to communicate what *was* thought by his or any tribe, but because he seeks to think *now* as the old ones thought *then.* (Whether he succeeds in this or not is the clue to the bi-religious character of his own thought, but the demonstration of this would be too elaborate to undertake here.) Deloria, unlike Storm, is not telling stories, old or new; he is extrapolating the conviction of the tribes in the light of his own critical analysis of them, and he is forcefully and persuasively setting out the results of this process for all who have ears to hear. To the extent that he succeeds in this his work is open to treatment from the standpoint of those who share his concerns but not all of his conclusions. Close in, this is the realm of emerging red theological discourse. Farther out, it is the realm of a theology in red, white, and black, and all which that portends. What is taking place in our time, before our eyes, is the movement of red religious reflection from an oral to a written tradition. Such a movement presses inexorably into the realm of historical understanding. In this sense Deloria cannot effect the total "relinquishing of temporal attitudes" for which we have seen him plead so effectively.[67]

The fact is that Deloria's is not the only way to be trans-tribal in the present. The decisive debate between Christians and those holding the ground he has taken will unfold first, and most significantly, *within* the tribal context itself. This conclusion is inescapable when one reflects on the most meaningful of the many citations in *God Is Red*, the words of a Sioux, Chief Luther Standing Bear, uttered "nearly half a century ago."

> The white man does not understand America. He is too far removed from its formative processes. The roots of the tree of his life have not yet grasped the rock and soil. The white man is still troubled by primitive fears; he still has in his consciousness the perils of this frontier continent, some of its fastnesses not yet having yielded to his questing footsteps and inquiring eyes. He shudders still with the memory of the loss of his forefathers upon its scorching deserts and forbidding mountaintops. The man from Europe is still a foreigner and an alien. And he still hates the man who questioned his path across the continent.

But in the Indian the spirit of the land is still vested; it will
be until other men are able to divine and meet its rhythm.
Men must be born and reborn to belong. Their bodies must
be formed of the dust of their forefathers' bones.[68]

These words relate to *all* red brothers and sisters, Christians
and non-Christians alike. Those of the tribal world who
have embraced the Christian faith and are not about to
renounce it are not foreigners and aliens in this land. Their
bodies, too, are formed of the dust of their forefathers'
bones, and the embracing of the gospel of Jesus the Christ
does not alter this. In them, too, the spirit of the land is still
vested. The heritage they share with those who reject the
Christian faith cannot be undone. On this side of the rise of
America's ethnic revolutions, one can no longer fail to
recognize one fact: Red Christians have more in common
with those who see the trail to tomorrow in the religions of
the tribes than they have with those who share with them
the Christian faith but who (contradictorily) deny the red
right to tribal identity. Can the symbols of the Christian
faith make peace with those encountered in this land? We
will know only when red Christian theologians answer. The
obstructions in their way have at last begun to collapse.

There is a proleptic character to the work of Deloria, and
in this resides the fact that he, just as Wilmore, exemplifies
the parameter of *mutual openness to change.* His argument
not only can be debated, it yearns for recognition as a full
participant in the realm of reciprocal creativity, both within
the tribal context and beyond it. For red Christians as well
as for Deloria himself, God is red in the profound sense in
which he uses this phrase. For others who dwell in this
land, who have never known any other home, but who only
now are beginning to grasp what it means to be at home in
America, the sense in which this is true for them too awaits

deepening clarification. Both for them and for Deloria the sharing of a new future offers the only possibility of the glad celebration of diversity. He, too, exemplifies the quality described by the parameter of mutual openness to change, for he too envisions a world that cannot be real without it.

C. White Theology:
Liberation Into Particularity

The crisis of theology in America's white community is the crisis of rebirth—always traumatic, always a wrenching, always a transmutation into a new reality. Liberation is at hand for the white theological world, as well as for the red and the black. It is liberation into particularity. The gospel of Jesus the Christ transcends all histories, and it does so by being capable of statement in terms of each. When the heirs of the vast, multifaceted tradition of Western theological reflection know themselves to comprise only one of the composites of the full mosaic that is humanity, they begin to become—*white*. White theology must take its place *alongside* red theology and black theology, laboring on a par with them, hoping and working for the day when brown theology and yellow theology shall complete the full mosaic, and struggling to cancel out the dominance of the North Atlantic Theology—whence it comes—by bringing that tradition into the red/white/black triangle and placing it at the disposal of an emergent new future. This book as a whole is an attempt to function in this way. Both the argument that we have followed and the voices—*all* of them—that we have heard can help us now to discern and sharpen how this must be carried forward in a context where all involved must be characterized by mutual openness to change.

The heart of the matter is the problem of analogy, the

problem of language, which is always present where
theology is seriously attempted. Fundamentally, analogies
have to do with similarities and correspondences, with
resemblances and agreements, with parallels and affinities.
How does one speak about God, how does one order and
communicate the search for ultimacy, in human language,
the language of the world of man and woman? How does
one select the words that most meaningfully symbolize the
similarity and correspondence between the ultimate reality
that is God and the human reality that yearns for this
ultimacy? The problem of theology's use of analogy has a
history that is convoluted with manifold, tortuous, labyrin-
thine paths, because it is the history of this selectivity, and
its key turning points are correlated with decisive shifts in
the contours and sources of its imagery. Theology is always
faced with the task of disciplining the unending possibilities
of analogical imagination.

Two high moments in the history of theology have
involved explicit indication of how this disciplining is to be
effected. The thought of Thomas Aquinas turns on the
analogia entis, the analogy of being; the thought of Karl
Barth turns on the *analogia fidei,* the analogy of faith. We
might express it thus: Thomas argued that *being*-words must
be normative in the theological discourse; Barth argued that
faith-words alone will suffice. Now it is instructive that
Barth, in the process of unfolding the yield of the analogy of
faith, across the broad sweep of his *Church Dogmatics,* was
ultimately driven to pick up and bend to his own use the
perceptive cogency of an insight of his youthful contemporary, Dietrich Bonhoeffer. This was Bonhoeffer's suggestion
of the *analogia relationis,* the analogy of relationship. In
effect, Bonhoeffer insisted that only *relational* words can
supply the vocabulary needed for theological reflection, and
this insight is indeed one of the decisive clues to the

unfolding of his life and thought.[69] Now a powerfully new suggestion has arisen in the American context. This is Frederick Herzog's proposal of the *analogia liberationis,* the analogy of liberation, the insistence that *liberation*-words alone can do justice both to the thrust of the gospel of Jesus the Christ and to the context within which theology must now labor.

The way for white theology to become white—the way for it to take up its work as *one* component of the mosaic that is humanity—is to follow out the full implications of Herzog's *analogia liberationis* in its understanding of the Bible, its understanding of the history of theology throughout the two millenia of its development, its understanding of the new emergence of red and black theologies, and its understanding of its own involvement in the context of ethnic pluralism. Theology in this context *is* theology under the discipline of the analogy of liberation. The analogy of liberation is the necessary specification of the analogy of relationship when and where the world of human interrelationships is dominated by the fact of ethnic oppression and the struggle for release from it. To see why this is so we must first grasp what Herzog means by the proposal, and then formulate how this must be extended and refined in the context of the red/white/black triangle.

Frederick Herzog's *Liberation Theology* (1972) is subtitled *Liberation in the Light of the Fourth Gospel.* Herzog, who is professor of systematic theology at Duke University Divinity School, notes at the outset of his preface that the book was occasioned by a "strange coincidence" in 1970, the publication of James Cone's *A Black Theology of Liberation* within months of the publication of his own essay entitled "Theology of Liberation." Herzog wrote: "That in a time of particular racial stress both a black and a white could hit upon a common theme gave me pause for thought." [70] The work at hand, he goes on to indicate, represents both an expansion of the essay and the culmination of work on the Gospel of John which had occupied his attention for some years. Why the Fourth Gospel? For Herzog this Gospel "functions as interpretive key to liberation history," for "in the Fourth Gospel we can almost touch with our hands the first full-fledged theological wrestling with Jesus of Nazareth as liberator." [71]

Intrinsic to Herzog's understanding of Jesus as liberator, and thus to his insistence on the necessity of the analogy of liberation, is a central assumption that pervades his commentary as a whole: "Liberation—this is not a segment of the theological subject matter, but our historical space." [72] In saying this he is commencing the process of taking deadly aim at what he calls "the Cartesian self," the self that emanates from the famous *cogito, ergo sum* ("I think, therefore I am"), the individualistic self, whose outlook is endemic to the white world. Herzog refuses to use the term "white" in any positive sense, and from the viewpoint of our own discussion, as we shall demonstrate presently, this must be challenged. But, as will be seen, our challenge is one that completely concurs in Herzog's identification of the issue immediately at hand. What Herzog asserts is the necessity of a radical shift in the perspective informing the bulk of the theological effort of the contemporary white world. Crucial to such a shift is insight into what kind of *self* must be involved in the doing of theology:

> Obviously the self is involved in all that theology is about. The question is, *what kind* of self we focus on, and whether the self-certainty of a particular kind of self, the Cartesian self, is capable of carrying the whole weight of theology, as it were, on its shoulders. If I turn from the private self to the oppressed as part of the self, I am subjecting myself to a more primary hermeneutical or interpretive presupposition

operative in my theological thought, more primary because it has placed itself there *before* I begin to reflect on it in terms of my bourgeois self. *The oppressed as part of the self,* this is a compelling factor because of the power of the originating event of Christianity over us. And this happens within a corporate self—the community of the church. Here I learn that there are injustices I cannot forget.[73]

Herzog has no doubt whatsoever about the nature of the "originating event of Christianity." It has to do with "the identification of Jesus Christ with the wretched of the earth," an identification which involves more than the "freedom of the individual" since it gives him "public space for freedom to become operative." [74] Relentlessly, throughout the whole of his commentary, Herzog insists on the controlling centrality of this understanding of the originating event of Christianity. No facet of the Fourth Gospel fails to come alive with new intelligibility when it is considered in these terms.

Jesus himself belongs to the *marginales,* the forgotten, the nobodies. It is exactly where the glory of humanity is least obvious that it appears in its true power. We dare never forget the identity of Jesus with the marginal figures of life. It is here that corporate selfhood breaks forth. And it is *in the ability to identify with the forgotten, the nobodies, that we can check out the truth as to what Jesus was about.*[75]

The perspectival shift for which Herzog contends, and the understanding of Jesus as liberator, which is both its yield and its source, combine to produce a treatment of the midnight conversation between Jesus and Nicodemus that typifies the thrust of the commentary as a whole, and that contains one of its most memorable clarifications. Herzog translates the opening lines of John, ch. 3, as follows:

[1] Nicodemus, one of the Pharisees, a leader of the Jews, [2]came to Jesus by night. He said, "Rabbi, we know that you

are a teacher sent from God. No one can do the signs you do
unless God is with him." [3] Jesus answered, "Believe me, no
man can see the kingdom of God unless he becomes black."
[4] Nicodemus wondered, "How can a man become black
when he is white? Can he again enter his mother's body and
be born different?" [5] Jesus said, "Believe me, if a person is
not born of water and Spirit he cannot enter the kingdom of
God. [6] Flesh creates flesh, and spirit creates spirit. [7] Do not
be surprised that I told you, you must become black. [8] The
wind blows where it wills. You hear the sound of it, but you
do not know where it comes from and where it goes. So it is
with everyone born of the Spirit." [76]

The crucial point in Herzog's reflections on this scene is
contained in his paraphrase of John 3:3, in which Jesus'
demand for rebirth is focused. The issue is that "Man needs
to go through the shock of recognition that he does not want
to change." [77] This is what Herzog seeks to emphasize by
having Jesus demand of Nicodemus that he must *become*
black. At this point he is explicitly putting to use a key idea
of James Cone's, one with which we are already familiar,
and in so doing he is specifying the manner in which his
own perspectival suggestion becomes concrete.

> To become black means to give up one's glamorous white
> self-image. "Blackness is an ontological symbol and a visible
> reality which best describes what oppression means in
> America" (James H. Cone). We could also speak of redness
> as an ontological symbol of oppression. The Indian too is
> debased. To be freed is always a question of being enabled
> to identify with the *marginales,* the people on the borders of
> society, through the power of the one who started doing it.
> Through Jesus we are able to enter the kingdom of God (v.
> 3), the realm in which all men are free as the truly free man
> rules over all. To worship one's beautiful private self is
> enslavement. To be related to corporate selfhood through
> Jesus is freedom.[78]

The concreteness insisted upon is not rooted in human contrivance, but in God's act. This, for Herzog, is the central thrust of the Fourth Gospel.

> The blackness or redness of the man reborn is always related to *Jesus'* blackness or redness. It is always *his* kind of blackness or redness that counts. It is not *our* identification, but *his* identification with the wretched of the earth that counts and brings the great change among men. Therefore it is always called a rebirth *through the Spirit.* It is a gift mediated through the Jesus event (v. 5). Man needs to be reminded time and again that of his own accord he does not want to find liberation of consciousness through this event.[79]

All that we now have before us combines to yield Herzog's proposal of the analogy of liberation. The idea not only crystallizes his contribution as a whole, it also makes good the claim he enunciates at the outset of his introduction to the work: "This is a book on the reordering of theological priorities." [80] His is not the first theological treatise to take on the burden of attempting to shift the direction of the whole theological tradition, and it will not be the last, but he is one of those rare theologians who is willing to assert, whatever the risk, the full implication of what he is proposing.

> Once man grasps corporate freedom he is on the way to becoming man. On his own, man remains in the state of concealment. It takes an act of liberation—responded to by faith—to unshackle us from our self-contradiction. Only through liberation from the concealment of privatism can we be set on the road to becoming human. This occurs in the unconcealed one who uncovers the new direction of our destiny toward a new future: "So if the Son liberates you, you will be free indeed" [John 8:36]. As for the *Reformation* justification by faith was the interpretive key to the Christian life; for the *Liberation* today, liberation by the Son is the key.

This is the core thought of the Fourth Gospel of our age. Man can only be grasped through the analogy of liberation (*analogia liberationis*), in accord with his liberation in Christ. Man is not something static, finished, but a process of ever-increasing freedom, a growth into greater freedom.[81]

Such, then, is Herzog's case for the claim that *liberation* words must be normative for the theological enterprise. The vocabulary of liberation is crucial to both the gospel and the attempt to explicate it precisely because humanity is not static and finished but is caught up in a process of ever-increasing freedom. How open is Herzog's analogy of liberation—open enough to undergo extension and refinement in the context of theology in red, white, and black? Open enough to know the discipline of that triangulation which such a theology entails? Open enough to be read *alongside* the thought of Wilmore *and* Deloria? Open enough to be exemplary of *mutual openness to change* just as the yield of the arguments of each of them is?

The issue at hand cannot be avoided, for we are deliberately bringing Herzog's analogy of liberation into the framework of our own discussion in a way that at first glance would seem to contravene his very point of departure. He does not introduce the demand of *becoming black* with the discussion of John, ch. 3, but rather at the outset of the preface to his commentary!

Crucial to my argument is the judgment of the oppressed on our white affluent ways. There will be violent disagreement with the idea that we must "become black": the demand of the hour is for whites to become white; we cannot become what we are not! But I do not know how else to call attention to the need for theology to begin with a radical *metanoia*. As long as we predicate Christian existence on our old white ways we will be denying our Lord.[82]

How radical a *metanoia* (change) is at stake for a theology of liberation that must embrace the *full range* of the problematic of American's ethnic revolutions? Surely Herzog does not intend an abstract reduction in the following formulation (at the end of his reflections on John 3:1–21)— but in the light of all that we have seen that is how it must be construed if it is left as it stands:

> To be reborn, to become black (or Indian, or Vietnamese peasant, or Soviet Jew), is thus to find a new selfhood. Jesus offers it: "Light has entered the world" (v. 19). In him man already is the new man. He who trusts him enters into new community—which is ultimately the realm of liberation, "the kingdom of God" (vv. 3–5). In the community of the church man receives in liberation a foretaste of the kingdom.[83]

The fact is that oppression and the experience of it is not unilinear; it is complex, it is plural. One cannot think black and think red at the same moment without doing violence to one or the other. And so the road to inexhaustible freedom for whites involves becoming neither black nor red, but *white*, for the first time. It involves becoming white as liberated into particularity, the particularity of being *one* component in the full mosaic that is humanity; becoming white in such a way that white cannot be white unless red and black are equally present in the historical space that is human liberation; becoming white in such a way that even along with red and black the triangle is a fragment, hoping and working for transmutation into the pentagram that is red, white, black, brown, and yellow. No reduction of the dynamics of the experience that is oppression and liberation from it can survive the plural creativity which the unleashing of the analogy of liberation inexorably generates. As Wilmore intensifies Cone's proclamation by moving deeper than blackness as an ontological symbol, and as Deloria insists that only if God is red can the tribes know either their ancient heritage or the gospel or both, so must we contend that the liberation of the gospel for whites involves becoming white in ways no living memory enshrines, for it involves whiteness as one *ethnic* component among the sweep of five. Liberation is inexhaustibly plural, because the corporate selfhood, for which we have seen Herzog plead, is intrinsically diverse.

In saying all this, however, we have only *apparently* contradicted Herzog, for no such reduction as we have challenged can be long maintained by an argument such as he has developed. Indeed, the very word "open" lies at the heart of his commentary since it informs the epitome of his Christology. This is explicit in his treatment of the conversation between Jesus and the Samaritan woman (John 4:1–45).

> In the open man, discrimination becomes pointless. . . .
> The walls of discrimination, the external barriers of national, racial, and class distinctions no longer keep men apart from each other in the open man. In him personhood is the final criterion. In speaking to the Samaritan woman, Jesus was doing what according to man's corporate self is the thing to do. He simply confronts the other person. And he identifies with the wretched of the earth, the outcast.[84]

What the *open man* brings is the new recognition of the concrete situation of plural humanity, for he is an *inclusive* event in the history of humanity.

> The open man is an inclusive event in the history of mankind. . . . In the story the Samaritan and the Jew are liberated. They find a new freedom in their relationship to each other. Thus the man called Jesus is the liberator of the world (vv. 39–42). . . . What is important to remember in

this passage is that the open man brings about a new concrete situation by simply confronting men in their separateness. . . . "The problem of the twentieth century is the color-line," Du Bois said decades ago. Here we see what it means. The need for liberation becomes clear at the color-line. Freedom does not break forth in immediate reconciliation. It grows out of the open clash in polarization, as men are liberated to participation in corporate selfhood.[85]

To extend the analogy of liberation as we must, by submitting it to the discipline of theology in red, white, and black, is not to counter Herzog. It is rather to take his suggestion with the utmost seriousness—to take it forward, that is, in the name of the Open One. It is fitting to culminate our discussion of Herzog with his own citation of the words of Du Bois with which we began. For with these words now in direct proximity with the gospel itself an effort to understand the inexhaustible claim of the Christian faith is at hand which must run beyond all prior white efforts to grasp it. Herzog, like Wilmore and Deloria, can only be read as exemplary of mutual openness to change, for he too envisions a world that cannot be real without it.

D. *Conclusion*

Considered as a mark of theology in the context of ethnic pluralism, the parameter of mutual openness to change is intrinsically a matter of *praxis*. That is, it can only be discerned in operation. Its delineation presupposes the continuing ferment of the processes of mutual intelligibility and mutual interdependence, combining in such a way that reciprocal creativity, with all the variety of fluctuating tempos it entails, inexorably drives toward ever widening horizons of involvement and insight. It is, in fact, yielded ever anew by what it helps to happen. Its relationship to the other three marks of theology in red, white, and black, is symbiotic. It lives only as they live; they live only if it does.

To have begun the process of moving completely around the red/white/black triangle is to have begun to understand what it means to say this. From *all* sides of the triangle insights abound that cannot know true fulfillment apart from the pluralism as a whole. This is no less the case for the longstanding white tradition than it is for the new developments on the expanding fronts of red and black theological creativity. To be sure, the far-reaching implications of the ideas from Troeltsch, Barth, and Tillich with which we have been concerned know a forcefulness all their own, but surely it must be acknowledged that in the process of theological triangulation, in which we have been involved, these mighty conclusions discover new depths and new usefulness. And as we have seen, the thought of Herzog can only know its true fulfillment if it is carried beyond the black/white exchange into the red/white/black triangle, and as this itself transmutes into the full panorama of theology in red, white, black, brown, and yellow, it can only be anticipated that his creativity will find further and more decisive extensions and applications.

From this emerges a categorical assertion that embodies not only the conclusion of this chapter but also the yield of this work as a whole. Identity in pluralism is superior to identity outside it. This is to bring the I-Thou principle into the *multilogical* world, so to say, for "dialogue" is too tame a word to indicate what we have been involved with in the red/white/black triangle. The only theology that can function in the multilogical world of ethnic pluralism is a theology of theologies. Put more sharply, this is to insist that no single confession of the gospel of Jesus the Christ can ever suffice. There can be no valid Christology unless there are valid Christologies. The intractable integrity of the multi-ethnic world in which humanity will always be cast both insists on and ensures this. The reverse is equally true. A singular Christology is intrinsically false, just as a singular theology is not only culturally myopic, but in fact idolatrous.

Mutual openness to change cannot be defined, it cannot even be described. It can only be *done*. If the reciprocal creativity it nourishes thrives, the most priceless of all dreams will stride further into reality. We should have known this long ago.

[31] Then Jesus told the Jews who trusted him, "If you continue to share my word, you are truly my disciples. [32] You will know the truth, and the truth will set you free." [John 8:31–32.] [86]

The sharing itself is the clue, for the Kingdom of God is a mosaic.

NOTES

Chapter 1. THEOLOGY AND HISTORIES

1. W. E. Burghardt Du Bois, *The Souls of Black Folk* (The New American Library, Inc., 1969 [originally published 1903], p. xi.

2. In saying this I am contending that *The Souls of Black Folk* (1903) must be understood as falling within the genre of autobiography, and this is of course debatable. To this I then add three works that clearly do unfold within this category: *Darkwater: Voices from Within the Veil* (1920); *Dusk of Dawn: An Essay Toward an Autobiography of a Race Concept* (1940); and *The Autobiography of W. E. B. DuBois: A Soliloquy on Viewing My Life from the Last Decade of Its First Century*, ed. by Herbert Aptheker (published posthumously; International Publishers Company, Inc., 1968).

3. Du Bois, *The Souls of Black Folk*, p. 274.

4. *Ibid.*, p. 276.

5. *Ibid.*

6. *Ibid.*, pp. 274–275.

7. The remark is controversial by design. Here I stand on my own study of the thought of Ernst Troeltsch (1865–1923), who was the first figure to wrestle at length with this issue. Cf. my *Toward a Theology of Involvement: The Thought of Ernst Troeltsch* (The Westminster Press, 1966), especially Chs. 5 and 6.

8. In speaking of "America" and of "American theology" in

this paragraph, and elsewhere throughout this discussion as a whole, I am referring to theological reflection in the context of the general situation in the United States. In so doing I am fully aware that this will be problematical, if not offensive, for many of those most in sympathy with what I am attempting in this book. Canadian brothers and sisters, as well as those from the Caribbean, Latin America, and South America, have every reason to be suspicious of the nationalism that accompanies the continued reduction of the term "America" to an equivalent for "the United States." As will become evident in the discussion, I trust, such is not what I intend. In the face of the demands on vocabulary which the argument in this discussion already entails I have been unable to find a way of helpfully solving this particular question. That the American scene (in the sense of the United States) is pervaded by racism (as thought of above) is the fact with which I wish to deal.

9. Phraseology such as this is beginning to become current, especially as the U.S. bicentennial year, 1976, comes closer. The use I am making of it reflects an idea of Vine Deloria, Jr.; cf. *infra*, p. 57.

10. Cf., e.g., the May–June 1969 issue of *Social Progress*, A Journal of Church and Society (United Presbyterian Church U.S.A.), Vol. LIX, No. 5, entitled "Viva La Raza." Cf. also Wesley S. Woo, "China and Chinese-American Identity," *China Notes* (East Asia Office, National Council of Churches, New York), Vol. XI, No. 4 (Autumn 1973), pp. 44–46 and David Ng, "The Chinaman's Chances Are Improving," *ibid.*, pp. 46–48.

11. Thus it is fragmentary in the sense that Paul Tillich championed. Cf. his *Systematic Theology*, Vol. III (The University of Chicago Press, 1963), p. 140.

Chapter 2. THE DISCIPLINE OF MUTUAL INTELLIGIBILITY

1. Benjamin A. Reist, *Toward a Theology of Involvement: The Thought of Ernst Troeltsch* (The Westminster Press, 1966), p. 194. (All citations from Troeltsch are my own translations, as originally

published in the work indicated, where details regarding the German texts are given. In the single instance where I have cited a passage not treated in that work I will give the sources of the passage here [cf. *infra*, n. 8].)

2. *Ibid.*, p. 199.

3. Cf. Adolf Harnack, *What Is Christianity?*, tr. by Thomas Bailey Saunders, intro. by Rudolf Bultmann (Harper & Brothers, 1957 [This English translation was originally published in 1901]).

4. Reist, *Toward a Theology of Involvement*, p. 185.

5. *Der Historismus und seine Probleme* was published in 1922 as Vol. III of Troeltsch's *Gesammelte Schriften;* I devote Chs. 3 and 4 of my study of his thought to the analysis of it.

6. Reist, *Toward a Theology of Involvement*, p. 60.

7. *Ibid.*, p. 65.

8. Ernst Troeltsch, *Der Historismus und seine Ueberwindung,* fünf Vorträge von Ernst Troeltsch, eingeleitet von Friedrich von Hügel-Kensington (Berlin: Pan Verlag Rolf Heise, 1924), pp. 69–70 (my translation); cf. *Christian Thought: Its History and Application*, ed. and with an introduction and index by Baron F. von Hügel (Meridian Books, Inc., Living Age Books, 1957), pp. 44–45.

9. Reist, *Toward a Theology of Involvement*, p. 199.

10. Vincent Harding, "The Afro-American Past," *New Theology No. 6*, ed. by Martin E. Marty and Dean G. Peerman (The Macmillan Company, 1969), p. 168. Originally published in *Motive*, April 1968, this is a slightly edited version of "The Uses of the Afro-American Past," in *The Religious Situation: 1969*, ed. by Donald R. Cutler (Beacon Press, 1969), pp. 829 ff., which itself was originally published in *Negro Digest*, Feb. 1968.

11. Vincent Harding, "Beyond Chaos: Black History and the Search for the New Land," *Amistad 1*, ed. by John A. Williams and Charles F. Harris (Random House, Inc., Vintage Books, 1970), p. 288.

12. *Ibid.*, p. 268.

13. Cf. *ibid.*, pp. 269, 275.

14. *Ibid.*, p. 278.

15. *Ibid.,* p. 279.

16. William Styron, *The Confessions of Nat Turner* (Random House, Inc., 1967; paperbound edition, The New American Library, Inc., Signet Books, 1968).

17. *William Styron's Nat Turner: Ten Black Writers Respond,* ed. by John Henrik Clarke (Beacon Press, Inc., 1968).

18. Vincent Harding, "You've Taken My Nat and Gone," in *ibid.,* pp. 23–33.

19. *The New York Review of Books,* Vol. XI, No. 4 (Sept. 12, 1968), pp. 34–37.

20. *Ibid.,* No. 8 (Nov. 7, 1968), p. 31.

21. Vincent Harding, "Beyond Chaos: Black History and the Search for the New Land," Williams and Harris, *loc. cit.,* p. 288.

22. *Ibid.,* p. 281.

23. *Ibid.,* p. 283.

24. *Ibid.,* pp. 283–284.

25. Vincent Harding, "The Religion of Black Power," *The Religious Situation: 1968,* ed. by Donald R. Cutler (Beacon Press, Inc., 1968), pp. 3–38.

26. *Ibid.,* p. 36.

27. *Ibid.,* p. 37.

28. *Ibid.,* p. 31.

29. *Ibid.*

30. *Ibid.,* p. 37.

31. Vine Deloria, Jr., *Custer Died for Your Sins: An Indian Manifesto* (Avon Books, 1970 [first published 1969]), p. 263.

32. *Ibid.,* pp. 267–268.

33. *Ibid.,* p. 183.

34. Vine Deloria, Jr., *We Talk, You Listen: New Tribes, New Turf* (The Macmillan Company, 1970), p. 88.

35. Deloria, *Custer Died for Your Sins,* p. 175.

36. *Ibid.,* p. 175.

37. *Ibid.,* p. 88.

38. *Ibid.,* p. 201.

39. Deloria, *We Talk, You Listen,* p. 16.

40. Deloria, *Custer Died for Your Sins,* p. 35.

41. *Ibid.*, p. 56.
42. *Ibid.*, p. 185.
43. *Ibid.*, p. 203.
44. Cf. Deloria, *We Talk, You Listen*, p. 148.
45. *Ibid.*, p. 145.
46. *Ibid.*, p. 147.
47. *Ibid.*
48. *Ibid.*, p. 152.
49. Deloria, *Custer Died for Your Sins*, p. 108.
50. *Ibid.*, p. 108–109.
51. *Ibid.*, p. 127.
52. Vincent Harding's phrase; cf. *supra*, p. 45.

Chapter 3. THE PROMISE OF MUTUAL INTERDEPENDENCE

1. Martin Buber, *I and Thou*, tr. by Ronald Gregor Smith (Edinburgh: T. & T. Clark, 1937), p. 3.
2. Karl Barth, *Die kirchliche Dogmatik*, III/2 (Zollikon-Zürich: Evangelischer Verlag A.G., 1948), pp. 264 ff.; cf. *Church Dogmatics*, Vol. III, Part 2, ed. by G. W. Bromiley and T. F. Torrance (Edinburgh: T. & T. Clark, 1960), pp. 222 ff. All of the following citations from Barth are my own translations; references to the German text are indicated by *KD*, III/2, which will be followed by references to the published English translation, indicated by *CD*, III/2, for those wishing to compare translations.
3. *KD*, III/2, pp. 295–296; cf. *CD*, III/2, pp. 247–248.
4. *KD*, III/2, p. 298; cf. *CD*, III/2, p. 250.
5. *KD*, III/2, p. 302; cf. *CD*, III/2, p. 252.
6. *KD*, III/2, p. 303; cf. *CD*, III/2, p. 253.
7. *KD*, III/2, p. 312; cf. *CD*, III/2, p. 260.
8. *KD*, III/2, p. 318; cf. *CD*, III/2, p. 265.
9. *KD*, III/2, p. 318; cf. *CD*, III/2, p. 265.
10. *KD*, III/2, p. 330; cf. *CD*, III/2, p. 274.
11. *KD*, III/2, p. 333; cf. *CD*, III/2, p. 277.
12. *KD*, III/2, p. 341; cf. *CD*, III/2, p. 283.
13. *KD*, III/2, p. 342; cf. *CD*, III/2, pp. 283–284.

14. Let it be understood, however, that by King's own account there were other decisive influences: Thoreau, Rauschenbusch, his own sense of debate with Marxism, the "personalism" of his teachers at Boston University School of Theology, Professors Brightman and DeWolf, and his own doctoral work on Hegel, all of which must be reckoned with in any definitive treatment of his thought. Cf. Martin Luther King, Jr., *Stride Toward Freedom: The Montgomery Story* (Harper & Brothers, 1958), especially Ch. VI, "Pilgrimage to Nonviolence."

15. King, *Stride Toward Freedom*, pp. 95–96.

16. *Ibid.*, pp. 96–97.

17. *Ibid.*, p. 102.

18. *Ibid.*, p. 103.

19. *Ibid.*, p. 102.

20. *Ibid.*, p. 106. (For King's elaboration of these insights in six points, cf. *ibid.*, pp. 102–106.)

21. *Ibid.*, pp. 98–99.

22. *Ibid.*, p. 99.

23. We touch on complicated matters here, of course. King was not the only decisive charismatic leader in this cause, and this was not the first time his leadership role was challenged. For a helpful beginning on this crucial story, cf. Coretta Scott King, *My Life with Martin Luther King, Jr.* (Holt, Rinehart & Winston, Inc., 1969), David L. Lewis, *King: A Critical Biography* (Frederick A. Praeger, Inc., Publishers, 1970), and the earlier and extremely perceptive discussion by Louis E. Lomax, *To Kill a Black Man* (Holloway House Publishing Co., 1968), with its remarkable comparison of the assassinations of King and Malcolm X.

24. Martin Luther King, Jr., *Where Do We Go from Here: Chaos or Community?* (Beacon Press, 1968), pp. 33 ff.

25. *Ibid.*, pp. 36 ff.

26. *Ibid.*, pp. 38 ff.

27. *Ibid.*, p. 44.

28. *Ibid.*, p. 48.

29. *Ibid.*, p. 62.

30. *Ibid.*, pp. 90–91.

31. Martin Luther King, Jr., *The Trumpet of Conscience* (Harper & Row, Publishers, Inc., 1968), p. 59 (cf. also *ibid.*, pp. 14–15).

32. *Ibid.*, p. 24.

33. *Ibid.*, pp. 74–75 (cf. King, *Stride Toward Freedom*, p. 217).

34. King, *Stride Toward Freedom*, p. 217.

35. *Ibid.*, p. 224.

36. King, *Where Do We Go from Here* . . . ? p. 191.

37. *Ibid.*, p. 22.

38. James H. Cone, *Black Theology and Black Power* (The Seabury Press, 1969), pp. 20–21.

39. *Ibid.*, p. 1.

40. *Ibid.*, p. 48.

41. For a crucial, explicit indication of this, cf. James H. Cone, *A Black Theology of Liberation* (J. B. Lippincott Company, 1970), p. 152.

42. *Ibid.*, p. 17 (Cone's italics).

43. *Ibid.*, p. 27, and p. 32, n. 5. I have here combined the phraseology of the text (p. 27) with that of the second of the key footnotes in which Cone works out this point (p. 32, n. 5). The first and more extensive note, which undergirds both formulations, is n. 4 on pp. 28–29.

44. Cf. *ibid.*, pp. 120, 152–154.

45. *Ibid.*, p. 185.

46. *Ibid.*, p. 184.

47. *Ibid.*, pp. 185–186.

48. *Ibid.*, p. 77.

49. *Ibid.*, p. 78.

50. *Ibid.*, pp. 77 ff.

51. *Ibid.*, p. 80.

52. *Ibid.*, pp. 79–80 (Cone's italics).

53. James H. Cone, *The Spirituals and the Blues: An Interpretation* (The Seabury Press, 1972), p. 147 (in the extensive note 5, pp. 146–147, which is related to the text on pp. 22–23 of Cone's book).

54. *Ibid.*, p. 101.

55. *Ibid.*, p. 106.

56. That he is continuing to work along this line is evidenced in his inaugural address as Professor of Theology at Union Theological Seminary, New York, "The Dialectic of Theology and Life, or Speaking the Truth," *Union Seminary Quarterly Review*, Vol. XXIX, No. 2 (Winter 1974), pp. 75–89.

57. In this connection, Winthrop D. Jordan's massive study, *White Over Black: American Attitudes Toward the Negro, 1550–1812* (Penguin Books, Inc., 1969), deserves close attention. It can be read as a remarkable demonstration of this point.

Chapter 4. SENSITIVITY TO VARYING RATES OF RELATABILITY

1. Frank Waters, *Book of the Hopi,* drawings and source material recorded by Oswald White Bear Fredericks (Ballantine Books, 1969 [first published, 1963]), p. xv.

2. Charles Alexander Eastman (Ohiyesa), *The Soul of the Indian: An Interpretation* (Houghton Mifflin Company, 1911), pp. 119–120. Cf. T. C. McLuhan, *Touch the Earth: A Self-Portrait of Indian Existence* (Outerbridge and Dienstfrey, distributed by E. P. Dutton & Co., Inc., 1971), p. 7.

3. Cf. *supra*, p. 60.

4. Vine Deloria, Jr., *God Is Red* (Grosset & Dunlap, 1973), p. 49.

5. *Ibid.*, p. 54.

6. *Ibid.*, p. 55.

7. Eastman, *op. cit.*, pp. 53–54.

8. *Ibid.*, p. 171.

9. Cf. Deloria, *God Is Red*, p. 102; McLuhan, *op. cit.*, p. 16; and John G. Neihardt, *Black Elk Speaks: Being the Life Story of a Holy Man of the Oglala Sioux,* as told through John G. Neihardt (Flaming Rainbow), illustrated by Standing Bear (University of Nebraska Press, A Bison Book, 1961 [first published, 1932]), p. x.

10. Neihardt, *op. cit.*

11. Cf., e.g., Neihardt, *op. cit.*, pp. 278–279.

12. Eastman, *op. cit.*, p. 21.

13. *Ibid.*, pp. 4–5.

14. *Ibid.*, p. 6.

15. I was first instructed regarding the depth and significance of the *vision quest* by Dr. Cecil Corbett, a Nez Percé Indian who is a United Presbyterian minister, and who currently serves as executive director of the Cook Christian Training School in Tempe, Arizona.

16. Eastman, *op. cit.*, p. 6.

17. *Ibid.*, pp. 6–8.

18. *Ibid.*, p. 78.

19. *Ibid.*, p. 13.

20. Deloria, *God Is Red*, p. 366.

21. Neihardt, *op. cit.*, p. 7.

22. *Ibid.*

23. *Ibid.*, p. viii.

24. Neihardt is an arresting figure in his own right. For details of his career as poet, professor, and journalist, cf. *ibid.*, p. 281.

25. For Neihardt's account of these meetings, cf. *ibid.*, pp. vii–xi.

26. *Ibid.*, p. 48.

27. *Ibid.*, p. 49.

28. *Ibid.*, pp. 20–47.

29. *Ibid.*, p. 28.

30. *Ibid.*, p. 29.

31. *Ibid.*, p. 30.

32. *Ibid.*, p. 45.

33. *Ibid.*, p. 34.

34. *Ibid.* The words in brackets are Neihardt's.

35. *Ibid.*, p. 37.

36. *Ibid.*, p. 38.

37. *Ibid.*, p. 43, n. 8.

38. *Ibid.*, pp. 42–43.

39. Waters, *op. cit.*, p. xxii.

40. *Ibid.*, p. 153.

41. Waters begins the fourth section of the *Book of the Hopi*

with this fascinating sentence: "The coming of the Hopis' lost white brother, Pahána, like the return of the Mayas' bearded white god, Kukulcan, the Toltecan and Aztecan Quetzalcoatl, was a myth so common throughout pre-Columbian America that we can regard it as arising from a concept rooted in the unconscious." (*Ibid.*, p. 307.)

42. *Ibid.*, p. 417. Cf. Waters' detailed discussion of the *kiva*, pp. 154–161, and also his illuminating commentary on "The Symbol of the Emergence," pp. 29 ff.

43. *Ibid.*, p. xvii.

44. *Ibid.*, p. 16.

45. There are others; cf. especially *ibid.*, pp. 29–30.

46. *Ibid.*, p. 17.

47. *Ibid.*

48. *Ibid.*, p. 18.

49. *Ibid.*

50. *Ibid.*, pp. 18–19.

51. *Ibid.*, p. 21.

52. *Ibid.*, p. 26. One continues to wonder what ancient memories are enshrined in this myth; for Waters' reflections, cf. *ibid.*, pp. 29–34.

53. *Ibid.*, p. 27.

54. Deloria, *God Is Red*, p. 366.

55. For what follows cf. Waters, *op. cit.*, pp. 14, 19, 22, 26, 27, 28.

56. Waters, *op. cit.*, p. 26.

57. *Ibid.*, p. 139.

58. Eastman, *op. cit.*, pp. 35–36.

59. *Ibid.*, pp. 88–89.

60. Paul Tillich, *Systematic Theology*, Vol. I (The University of Chicago Press, 1951), p. 8.

61. Paul Tillich, *Systematic Theology*, Vol. II (The University of Chicago Press, 1957), p. 13.

62. Tillich, *Systematic Theology*, Vol. I, p. 5.

63. For details, see Mircea Eliade, "Paul Tillich and the History of Religions," in Paul Tillich, *The Future of Religions*, ed. by Jerald C. Brauer (Harper & Row, Publishers, Inc., 1966), pp. 31 ff.

64. For details of its editing, see Tillich, *The Future of Religions,* pp. 7, 11.

65. Tillich, "The Significance of the History of Religions for the Systematic Theologian," in his *The Future of Religions,* p. 83. The address may also be found in *The History of Religions: Essays on the Problem of Understanding* (Essays in Divinity, Vol. I), ed. by Joseph M. Kitagawa *et al.* (The University of Chicago Press, 1967), pp. 241–255.

66. Tillich, *The Future of Religions,* p. 82.

67. *Ibid.,* p. 84.

68. *Ibid.*

69. *Ibid.*

70. *Ibid.,* p. 86.

71. *Ibid.*

72. *Ibid.,* pp. 86–87.

73. *Ibid.,* p. 87.

74. *Ibid.*

75. *Ibid.,* pp. 87–88.

76. *Ibid.,* p. 88.

77. *Ibid.,* p. 89.

78. *Ibid.*

79. *Ibid.,* p. 91.

80. *Ibid.*

81. *Ibid.,* p. 94.

Chapter 5. MUTUAL OPENNESS TO CHANGE

1. Gayraud S. Wilmore, *Black Religion and Black Radicalism* (Doubleday & Company, Inc., 1972), pp. xii–xiii. (His *The Secular Relevance of the Church* [1962] was published by The Westminster Press.)

2. Wilmore, *Black Religion and Black Radicalism,* pp. 298, 300, 302.

3. *Ibid.,* p. 5.

4. Cf. *ibid.,* p. 7.

5. *Ibid.,* p. 18 (cf. also pp. 22–23).

6. *Ibid.*, p. 300.

7. Cf. *ibid.*, pp. 87–101.

8. Cf. *ibid.*, pp. 53–54 ff.

9. *Ibid.*, p. 160.

10. *Ibid.*, p. 169.

11. *Ibid.*, p. 59.

12. *Ibid.*, p. 161.

13. *Ibid.*, p. 162. The statement quoted is from Edward Blyden, *Christianity, Islam and the Negro Race* (Aldine-Atherton, Inc., 1967), p. 45.

14. Wilmore, *Black Religion and Black Radicalism*, p. 291.

15. *Ibid.*, p. 295.

16. Cf. *supra*, p. 89.

17. Wilmore, *Black Religion and Black Radicalism*, pp. 295–296.

18. *Ibid.*, p. 296. Cone's actual words were: "Being black in America has very little to do with skin color" (Cone, *Black Theology and Black Power*, p. 151).

19. Wilmore, *Black Religion and Black Radicalism*, p. 296.

20. *Ibid.*

21. *Ibid.*, p. 297.

22. *Ibid.*, p. 298.

23. *Ibid.*

24. *Ibid.*, p. 299.

25. Cf., e.g., the impassioned book by Louis E. Lomax, *To Kill a Black Man* (1968), in which Lomax persuasively insisted on this within a year of King's assassination.

26. Wilmore, *Black Religion and Black Radicalism*, p. 242.

27. *Ibid.*, p. 245.

28. *Ibid.*, p. 250.

29. Cf. *ibid.*, p. 251.

30. Malcolm X (with the assistance of Alex Haley), *The Autobiography of Malcolm X* (Grove Press, 1965), pp. 200–201 (Malcolm's italics and punctuation throughout); quoted in Wilmore, *op. cit.*, p. 252.

31. Cf. Malcolm X, *op. cit.*, pp. 339, 362.

32. Wilmore, *Black Religion and Black Radicalism*, pp. 254–255.

33. *Ibid.*, p. 256 (Wilmore's italics).

34. Gayraud S. Wilmore, "The Black Church in Search of a New Theology," in Kendig B. Cully and F. Nile Harper, *Will the Church Lose the City?* (World Publishing Co., 1969), pp. 137–139.

35. Wilmore, *Black Religion and Black Radicalism*, p. 260.

36. Cf. Malcolm X, *op. cit.*, pp. 426–427.

37. Wilmore, *Black Religion and Black Radicalism*, p. 261.

38. Cf. *supra*, pp. 92–93.

39. Cf. *supra*, p. 96.

40. Wilmore, *Black Religion and Black Radicalism*, p. 297; cf. *supra*, pp. 152–153.

41. Cf. *supra*, pp. 109–110.

42. Cf. Vine Deloria, Jr., *God Is Red*, pp. 29 ff.

43. Cf. *ibid.*, pp. 37, 271.

44. Cf. *ibid.*, pp. 38, 257–258.

45. Cf. *ibid.*, pp. 54–55; cf. *supra*, pp. 106 ff.

46. Deloria, *God Is Red*, p. 69.

47. *Ibid.*, pp. 69–70.

48. *Ibid.*, pp. 73–74.

49. *Ibid.*, p. 74.

50. Cf., e.g., *ibid.*, pp. 225 ff.; and Ch. 13 as a whole, "Christianity and Contemporary American Culture" (noting carefully the governing note [*ibid.*, p. 315] concerning this chapter). Let no Christian protagonist protest these diatribes too quickly, for these images are communicated all too often by the Christianity of our time and place.

51. *Ibid.*, p. 127.

52. *Ibid.*, p. 137.

53. *Ibid.*, p. 138.

54. *Ibid.*, p. 166.

55. *Ibid.*

56. *Ibid.*, p. 128.

57. Cf. *ibid.*, pp. 139 ff., 311 ff. (n. 8).

58. Cf. *ibid.*, pp. 151 ff.

59. *Ibid.*, p. 153.

60. *Ibid.*, p. 129 (this is the title of Ch. 8 of *God Is Red*).

61. *Ibid.*, p. 268.

62. *Ibid.*, pp. 269–270.

63. Cf. *supra*, pp. 52–53.

64. Deloria, *God Is Red*, p. 287.

65. *Ibid.*, p. 301.

66. Cf. Storm's address to the reader, especially the closing section of it, with the careful instructions as to how the stories are to be used; in Hyemeyohsts Storm, *Seven Arrows* (Harper & Row, Publishers, Inc., 1972), pp. 4–11, especially pp. 10–11.

67. Deloria, *God Is Red*, p. 74; cf. *supra*, p. 165.

68. Deloria, *God Is Red*, p. 73 (originally in Luther Standing Bear, *Land of the Spotted Eagle* [Houghton Mifflin Company, 1933], p. 248; cf. Deloria, *op. cit.*, p. 308, n. 5).

69. Cf. my *The Promise of Bonhoeffer* (J. B. Lippincott Company, 1969), pp. 48 ff.

70. Frederick Herzog, *Liberation Theology: Liberation in the Light of the Fourth Gospel* (The Seabury Press, 1972), p. vii.

71. *Ibid.*, pp. ix–x.

72. *Ibid.*, p. ix.

73. *Ibid.*, p. 14 (Herzog's italics; in all citations that follow, the italics are Herzog's own).

74. *Ibid.*, p. 15.

75. *Ibid.*, p. 53.

76. *Ibid.*, p. 61 (the passage is John 3:1–8).

77. *Ibid.*, p. 63.

78. *Ibid.*, p. 64.

79. *Ibid.*, p. 65.

80. *Ibid.*, p. 1.

81. *Ibid.*, p. 126.

82. *Ibid.*, pp. vii–viii.

83. *Ibid.*, pp. 66–67.

84. *Ibid.*, p. 73.

85. *Ibid.*, pp. 77–78.

86. The translation is Herzog's (*op. cit.*, p. 125). He thus

ingeniously solves a fascinating problem. The Greek text for verse 31b reads, "If you [plural] continue in my word, you are truly my disciples." The question is, how does one underscore the drastic significance of the use of the second person plural here? Herzog does so with the marvelous phrase, "if you continue to share my word." At this point his argument and mine coincide.